MW01017450

FACING THE ENERGY CHALLENGE:
PERSPECTIVES IN CANADA AND THE UNITED KINGDOM

Titles of related interest from Ryburn include:

Environmental Issues:
the Response of Industry and Public Authorities
Proceedings of a Canada-United Kingdom Colloquium
Edited by D.K. Adams

Facing the Energy Challenge: Perspectives in Canada and the United Kingdom

Edited by D. K. Adams

Ryburn Publishing
KEELE UNIVERSITY PRESS

First published in 1993
by Ryburn Publishing
an imprint of
Keele University Press
Keele, Staffordshire

© British Committee
Canada-UK Colloquium
All rights reserved

Composed and printed by
Ryburn Publishing Services
Keele University, England

Contents

Preface and Acknowledgements

This volume is a record of the proceedings of a meeting of the Canada-UK Colloquium in Kananaskis, Alberta, Canada, in November 1992.

The Colloquium had its origins in intermittent meetings between concerned participants in the bilateral relationship between the United Kingdom and Canada in the 1970s and early 1980s. In the complexities of modern interstate relations both the Department of External Affairs in Ottawa and the Foreign and Commonwealth Office in London recognized the value of such a forum for the discussion of public policy issues of common concern. A more formal structure for the Colloquium was therefore established in 1986 with the creation of a British Committee. Since that time the British Committee has worked in partnership with Peter Dobell of the Institute for Research on Public Policy in Ottawa, and Colloquia have been held in successive years, alternating between venues in the United Kingdom and Canada.

Membership of the Colloquia embraces parliamentarians, officials, representatives of the business, financial, industrial and media communities, and academics. Financial support is given by DEA and the FCO, and each Colloquium has also enjoyed private sector sponsorship. Meetings are conducted under Chatham House rules, by which debates are privileged and freedom of speech protected. The formal presentations are, however, published, in order to give as wide a circulation as possible to the general policy issues discussed at each meeting. Themes for individual Colloquia are selected in terms of their immediate relevance to the two countries and engage issues of general public and political debate. Following a very successful meeting in Glasgow, in 1991, on *Environmental Issues: the response of Industry and Public Authorities* (published by Ryburn Publishing, 1993) it was decided that the 1992 Colloquium should address issues of energy, a logical succession given the interaction of environmental concerns and problems of carbon and nuclear emissions, and the public implications of contemporary governmental energy policies. The meeting was held at Kananaskis Village in the Canadian Rockies, in Alberta, and focused on supply and demand situations of energy industries, alternative energy sources, the role of government policies and regulation in energy strategies, the financial conditions of energy industries, and strategies for the future.

The experiment of an open Public Forum that was initiated at the Glasgow Colloquium, when members transferred to Dundee to address the local business and industrial community, was repeated in Canada. The Kananaskis group moved back to Calgary where four sessions were held, addressed by British presenters at Kananaskis. The level of discussion underlined the wider purposes of the Colloquium in widening the level of dialogue between the two countries.

Recognition is given to the Departments of External Affairs and Energy Mines and Resources, Ottawa, and to the Foreign and Commonwealth Office, London, for their financial support; to Mark Turner, Canada Desk Officer at FCO, for his total commitment to the interests of the Colloquium, to Vivien Hughes of the Canadian High Commission for her unwavering enthusiasm and application to detailed procedure, and to our Canadian associate, Peter Dobell, for his selection of the Canadian delegation, administrative arrangements at Kananaskis and in Calgary, and his devotion to the cause of trans-Atlantic understanding. Mr. Allan Hird, Executive Secretary of the British Committee, an essential member of the British team, was a pleasure to work with, and his administrative ability transformed the role of the chair.

Private sector sponsorship is fundamental to the workings of C-UKC, and for the 1992 Colloquium we are pleased to acknowledge the support of Amoco Canada Petroleum Co. Ltd, Shell Canada Ltd, Canadian Airlines International, the Canadian Energy Research Institute, and the Institute for Research on Public Policy.

The chair of the Kananaskis Colloquium was held by Senator Dan Hays, chair of the Canadian Senate Committee on Energy, Environment and Natural Resources. His long experience and wisdom not only facilitated debate but contributed immeasurably to the pursuit of issues. Sir Nicholas Bayne, British High Commissioner, Ottawa, attended, and contributed, to the discussion at Kananaskis, and gave the keynote speech in Calgary. Such participation at the highest level was of great value to the Colloquium.

In the preparation of this volume I am personally indebted to Amanda Gautby, secretary in the Department of American Studies at Keele, and to Richard Clark and Lucia Crothall of Ryburn Publishing.

D.K. Adams
Keele University
August 1993

1 Energy between Politics and Economics*

Nicholas Bayne

Introduction

The production and marketing of energy – such as coal, oil, gas and various forms of electrical power generation – is an economic activity, like manufacturing or banking or construction. Energy companies and utilities are concerned with economic objectives and economic laws, such as supply and demand, prices, investment decisions and return on capital.

But no area of civilian economic activity – not even agriculture – is so much a subject of intervention and regulation by governments. Governments too have economic objectives. But they also have other, more political aims: security of supply, protecting the consumer, preserving jobs, raising tax revenue or respecting environmental standards. Energy policy can be pulled one way by politics and another by economics. The current debate on the coal industry in Britain is a very striking example of this. Economics argue for closing mines, politics for keeping them open.

This tension in energy policy can be aggravated by conflicting international and domestic pressures. In the energy field, economic decisions are increasingly made on international criteria. Governments have dwindling control over what economic activities take place on their territory, because these can always move elsewhere. But they face persistent political demands from vulnerable groups within their country to protect them against external threats. The British coal mines issue illustrates this again. Hitherto British mines have had a guaranteed market through sales of coal to power stations. Part of the controversy has arisen because they now face increased external competition from imported coal.

But politics and economics are not fated always to pull in opposite directions. The most successful policies are those where governments can get economic and political factors to pull in the same direction and be mutually reinforcing. I want to examine three areas of energy policy to see how this mutually reinforcing effect can be achieved. I have chosen policy issues where the tensions arise as much from foreign policy as from

---

* This is the text of the address given by Sir Nicholas Bayne at the Calgary Petroleum Club on 11 November 1992. The opinions expressed are his own, and should not be taken as official government policy.

domestic pressures, so that, as a diplomat, I have something to say about them. One set of issues became critical in the 1970s, one in the 1980s and one is upon us now in the 1990s.

On each issue, I offer some personal reflections, based on my experience with the economic summit meetings of the G7 powers, in which both Britain and Canada have been much involved. I would not suggest the summits have been more successful than other channels in finding solutions to international energy problems. But when an issue appears on the summit agenda, that means both that the G7 governments are deeply worried about it and that they realize the need to reconcile domestic and international pressures.

Political Instability in the Middle East

My first issue, which became critical in the 1970s, is the political instability in the Middle East and the security of supplies of oil.

Everyone will recall the first oil crisis of 1973/74. This was the reaction by the Arabs to their defeat by Israel in the Yom Kippur war of October 1973. A brief period of interruption of oil supplies from the Middle East led into a fourfold expansion in the price of oil, from $3 to $12 per barrel. After much initial confusion, the political reaction of the main industrial powers was quite extensive. A new institution, the International Energy Agency (IEA), was created and continues to do good work to this day. President Giscard of France saw the need for a coordinated economic response to the first oil crisis. He made this the motive for calling together the first Western economic summit at Rambouillet in 1975.

But the economic response did not match the political efforts. Governments tried to shelter their populations from the consequences of high oil prices. As a result, consumption of oil and other forms of energy continued to grow, particularly in the US. Inflation accelerated dangerously; and the West was all too vulnerable to the second oil crisis which struck in 1978/79, provoked by the fall of the Shah and the arrival of Ayatollah Khomeini in Iran. This caused spot market prices almost to triple between October 1978 and June 1979, from $13 to $36. The rationing system put in place by the IEA did not really work. It took only a small shortfall in supply, about 5%, to provoke a scramble for available cargoes which drove up prices very steeply.

But this time the economic and political responses from the West were more consistent, though they took some time to work out. Energy issues dominated the G7 summits of 1979 and 1980. This time round the leaders realized that they must let the full effect of higher world oil prices work through their economies, and be reflected in higher domestic prices and lower demand. That was the only way of reducing the vulnerability of the OECD economies to repeated shocks of this kind. All the G7 countries agreed to follow this course – with one exception. That was Canada, where Prime Minister Trudeau did not follow the recommendations of his colleagues to allow domestic energy prices to rise to the same level of world prices. In so doing, I believe he made himself very unpopular in Alberta; I have heard some Albertans say that they consider themselves to be $50 billion poorer as a result.

The political response to the second oil crises focussed on various collaborative measures to limit imports, to find alternative sources of supply for oil and to develop alternative types of energy, especially coal, nuclear and synthetic fuels. All these were moves in the right direction. In practice the drop in demand for all types of energy brought about by the economic strategy meant that many of the targets set were never directly tested.

However, the resilience of the western economies has been demonstrated in other ways. Since 1979 there have been two more major political upheavals in the Middle East, which could well have produced the third and fourth oil shocks. The first was the Iran/Iraq war, which broke out in the autumn of 1980. The second was the Iraqi invasion of Kuwait and the ensuing Gulf War. Both of these involved reductions of about 5% of oil supplies to OECD countries, the same as the second oil crisis.

In late 1980, with world demand low and oil stocks high, it was possible to absorb the effect of the Iran/Iraq war by drawing down stocks and discouraging purchases in the spot market. The Gulf crisis of 1990/91 had a more dangerous initial impact, driving up oil prices from $20 per barrel in September 1990 to nearly $40 in October. But Saudi Arabia was able to mobilize additional supplies,to make good the shortfall from Iraq and Kuwait, and prices soon declined to more normal levels. The IEA helped by encouraging the release of stocks early in 1991, just before the allied attack of Iraq began. It would have been even better, in my view, if the IEA had released stocks the previous autumn. This could have prevented the surge in price and reduced the damage done at the time to some weaker economies.

We have thus survived the 1980s and early 1990s without an oil supply crisis provoked by political instability in the Middle East. But it could still happen again. On the economic side, world oil consumption, after falling off in the early 1980s, has now climbed back past its peak of 1978, fed especially by strong demand in Asia. Despite recent discoveries elsewhere, two thirds of the world's proven reserves of oil are in the Middle East. Politically, the Middle East remains an unstable region, with the growth of Islamic fundamentalism. The most hopeful sign is the progress being made, at long last, towards a settlement of the dispute between Israel and its Arab neighbours. If that could be resolved, the underlying political threat to oil supplies from the region would be greatly reduced, if not wholly removed.

Protecting the Environment

My second issue, which became critical in the 1980s, is concern with protecting the environment. This had already surfaced as an international issue as early as the Stockholm environment conference of 1972. But it was then submerged by the oil crises and ensuing recessions and only came back on to the agenda in the mid-1980s. The first time it was treated by a G7 summit was in London in 1984. By the Paris summit of 1989, it had become the issue to which the assembled leaders devoted the greatest amount of time and it has featured strongly since.

Not all environmental issues concern energy. But it is the energy related ones, such as air pollution from power stations and car exhausts, the escape of radio-activity into the atmosphere and most especially the greenhouse effect, which have the widest international impact. Acid rain or the radioactive clouds from Chernobyl respect no borders. The global warming produced by mounting levels of man-made CO_2 in the atmosphere is an issue which affects the future of the entire planet and human life on it. The policies of large, poor and populous countries like China, India and Brazil can have as much impact on global warming as those of rich industrialized countries.

Before the G7 and other developed countries could offer any recommendations to the rest of the world, they needed to work out their own strategy, to offer an example to others. Initially western governments, especially in Europe, tried to combat air pollution and reduce emissions of greenhouse gasses by regulation, prohibition and administrative measures. But this would have led to great tension between political and economic pressures. Even if it had worked in the West, it would not have been acceptable in the developing world. On reflection, western governments, in addition to administrative controls, are trying to make more use of prices and other economic levers to achieve environmental aims. This approach respects the 'pollution pays' principle; it tries to have the environmental costs reflected in the price of different forms of energy; and uses taxes and subsidies to encourage the shift towards more environmentally acceptable types of fuel.

In some ways the energy policy trends provoked by the oil crises have been useful in dealing with environmental pressures. Governments are already seeking to save energy and make their economies less energy dependent. These policies also help them to meet their targets for reducing emissions of greenhouse gasses.

The oil crises also encouraged a move away from oil to alternative fuels: to gas, nuclear power and coal. The 1980 summit, for example, called for no more oil-fired power stations but a doubling in the use of coal by 1990. Environmental factors have produced quite a different ranking. *Oil* is acceptable again. *Gas* is even more favoured as producing more energy for less CO_2 emissions. Gas has become very attractive for power stations; a Canadian consortium is building a new gas-fired station in Britain, east of London. *Nuclear power* has become more controversial then ever. Some environmentalists favour it as producing energy with no emissions of greenhouse gasses at all. Others point to the appalling danger of radioactive leaks. My impression is that the greatly increased security now required of nuclear power stations puts them at an economic disadvantage.

Coal is the fuel that has lost most ground for environmental reasons. In addition to releasing sulphur dioxide into the atmosphere, coal is only half as efficient as gas in relation to greenhouse gas emissions. Partly for environmental reasons, decisions on coal have produced political repercussions both in Canada and Britain. The dispute in Britain over the future of the coal industry has led to a comprehensive review of energy policy. Canada has suffered the tragedy of the Westray mine explosion in Nova Scotia. The mine was known to be extremely dangerous, but was reopened because the Westray coal was environmentally very efficient.

So it has been hard for the developed countries to work out their own environmentally acceptable energy policies, which can reconcile economic and political pressures. But these policies also have to find favour in the developing world, whose prospects are entirely different. It is not difficult for rich industrial economies to find ways of saving energy. But countries at the beginning of their development need to expand their energy capacity to power new industries. They will not readily agree that environmental factors should hold back their economic development. They will insist on being involved in working out any international regime.

That is why international discussion has to take place through United Nations channels, so that every country can have its say. This discussion reached a climax at the Rio Conference in June this year, which was the largest gathering of heads of state and government hitherto on record. The Rio conference is only the beginning of a series of negotiations on environmental issues, which will stretch well into the next century. But Rio established some basic principles which will determine what happens next.

There was a danger that at Rio developing countries would adopt a politically confrontational approach, blaming all the problems on the industrial countries and demanding to be paid for any environmental measures they took. But this view did not prevail. Both rich and poor countries were prepared to subscribe to an international climate change convention, which obliges each country to draw up a national strategy for keeping greenhouse gas emissions in check. Developing countries recognized that it was in their interest as well to preserve the world in a fit state for future generations. The developed countries accepted an obligation to help developing countries achieve their environmental strategies in ways which did not hold up their economic growth. A new financial instrument, the Global Environment Facility, was created to help developing countries meet the incremental costs of respecting their obligations under the climate change and other conventions.

Some were disappointed at the outcome of the Rio conference. I myself find it extraordinary that so many countries were prepared to accept constraints on their present policies for the sake of future generations. Governments of both rich and poor countries sought to respond to the political imperatives of environmental protection by measures which made economic sense and did not distort energy markets.

The Transformation of the Soviet Union

My third issue, which has become critical as the 1990s begin, is the transformation of the former Soviet Union. The USSR has collapsed as a communist super power and broken up into its component republics. Each of them is trying to put in place an efficient democratic system and a working market-based economy. They all have a very long way to go.

The collapse of the Soviet Union, which preoccupies us all, is already having profound effects on the energy scene. During the 1980s the Soviet Union (as it then was), was the world's third largest producer of coal, after the United States and China. It was the world's largest producer of oil. It became the world's largest producer of natural gas, overtaking the United States, and possessing 38% of proven world reserves.

The collapse of the Soviet Union is already having adverse effects on security of supply and on the international environment. A serious shortfall in energy supplies to the East European countries is crippling their efforts at economic reform. Germany, Italy and France are linked with Russia by a natural gas pipeline network, which caused great controversy at the 1982 G7 summit. Now the gas supplies by this route, which have risen from 20 to 60 billion cubic feet over the 1980s, are at risk from production shortfalls in Russia and disputes over transit across Ukraine. In the environment, there has been deep concern about the safety of nuclear power stations in the former Soviet Union ever since the escape of radioactivity from Chernobyl in 1986. There are still power stations of the same or similar design in operation and the safety procedures are known to be inadequate. The danger of another nuclear accident remains high.

Everywhere in Russia and the other new states the old political and economic structures have crumbled away or are on the point of collapse. But new arrangements are slow to take root and gain acceptance and legitimacy. In Russia President Yeltsin and his economic team have many of the right ideas for reform, but they are struggling against mounting political as well as economic obstacles. In other new states the process of reform is only just beginning.

The West has the strongest possible political incentive to see democracy established and the market economy develop in these former communist states. We welcome the collapse of communism and the end of super-power confrontation. The last thing we want to see is the Soviet Union replaced by a group of states whose economies are disintegrating, where border disputes and civil wars are breaking out and where the existence of huge stocks of weapons are a persistent threat to security.

This issue has dominated the last three G7 summits, and the leaders met with Gorbachev in 1991 and Yeltsin this year. The British and Canadian governments have been prominent in the G7 in trying to help the Russians put into place both the institutions and the policies required for macro-economic stabilization, for monetary reform and for dealing with the debt overhang. We have been active too in humanitarian assistance, to prevent popular hardship undermining essential reforms. But alongside these efforts to transform government and public administration in Russia, we also have to encourage the growth of a private sector economy. Here, as with the other issues we need techniques which enable politics and economics to pull in the same direction.

The first steps towards future prosperity for Russia must lie in the transformation of its primary industries, in particular energy, mining and agriculture. Most secondary manufacturing industry in Russia is hopelessly uneconomic. The tertiary service sector is in its infancy. But the energy industries, which already produce the greater part of Russia's foreign exchange earnings, can provide the foundation for future economic growth.

The transformation of the energy industry in Russia and other states will be a huge task. Production facilities and the physical distribution network are antiquated and prone to breakdown and leakage. Energy pricing policy in Russia and the other states hardly exists, so that the use of energy is enormously wasteful. The damage to the environment, not only from dangerous nuclear power stations but from other forms of air and water pollution, is very extensive. Finally, while the Russians have been ready to admit private foreign capital into other parts of their economy, they have hesitated to lose control of energy and other national resources.

But Russia's energy resources, in particular its natural gas and oil, are of interest to western firms, as British, Canadian and other companies have shown. In the right conditions, they can earn profits. So the essential task is to create such conditions, which might encourage private energy investment into Russia and other energy-rich states of the former Soviet Union, such as Kazakhstan. For this, I suggest a number of elements are required:

– A clear understanding of where responsibility lies for decisions on energy investment, reinforced by a proper regime of contract law.

– Opportunities for foreign companies to take equity stocks in energy undertakings, with a workable system for generating foreign exchange earnings and for remitting profits.

– A market-related domestic pricing system for energy, for both firms and households, to cut down waste and release more quantities for export.

– Assurance of free movement between republics, with no trade barriers or interruptions in transit.

These elements depend on decisions by the Russians and other states themselves. Governments and indeed Western companies can provide essential advice and training. The Energy Charter now under negotiation should provide a helpful framework of acceptable practice. In addition, some government financial support for energy projects will be needed, for example in improving the safety of nuclear power stations. But the aim must be to avoid using public finance to meet needs for which private capital could be available.

Even in the energy sector, which contains grounds for hope, transforming the former Soviet system is bound to be a long and painful process. The Russians and other states start with many handicaps. They face serious dangers from hyper-inflation and economic depression. They will need all the help they can get, from governments, international bodies and the private sector alike. It strikes me that Canada, with its highly successful energy and resource based economy in a large sparsely populated land area, provides a good model to which the Russians and others could aspire.

Conclusion

I have examined three questions, each of which struck me as being the dominant international energy issue in three successive decades. None of these is definitely resolved. We cannot be sure that political upheaval in the Middle East will not again disrupt energy supplies, though we have some defences in place. The outlines of acceptable solutions for protecting the environment are just now emerging. With the former Soviet Union we are only beginning to understand the scale of the problems. All three continue to require an effort of cooperation, not only between governments but also between governments and the private sector, to ensure that political objectives are pursued by methods which make economic sense and vice versa.

2 Supply and Demand Situations of Energy Industries

I Comments on the Future of the Energy-Commodity-
Producing Industries

Gerry Angevine

Energy Demand

The performance of the energy-commodity-producing industries in coming years will depend on demand and price developments and on public policy in relation to the environmental aspects of energy resource development, production, and use.

Demand for crude oil, natural gas, coal and uranium will largely be a function of economic growth. The Canadian Energy Research Institute's (CERI) most recent report on the outlook for the world oil market assumes that we will witness recovery from recession in the industrialized countries in 1993 and that growth rates in the years to 2007 will be in the vicinity of those shown in Figure 1.

Figure 1 Economic Growth by Region
(Average Real GDP Growth Rates, %)

	1994–2007
Canada	3.4
United States	3.5
Western Europe	2.1
Eastern Europe	3.5
C.I.S	4.6
Mexico	4.5
Cen./South America	4.2
Japan	3.3
Asia Pacific	5.0
Asia Africa	3.8
Middle East	3.7

These growth rates, taken mostly from reports by the United States Department of Energy's Energy Information Administration, envisage steady growth of the global economy. As a consequence, demand for crude oil, natural gas, coal and uranium will also grow. There will not, however, be a one-to-one correspondence in the response of energy supply to overall economic growth. As evidence of this, the E/GDP ratio has been declining in the industrial countries since the oil price crisis of 1973 – reflecting improved efficiencies in energy production and use and other factors.

E/GDP Considerations

Canada's E/GDP ratio is greater than that of the United Kingdom and the other countries shown in Figure 2. This is largely the result of differences among Canada and other industrialized countries with regard to the energy supply situation and energy requirements. For example, compared to Japan, Canada is self-sufficient in energy. Because energy is readily available and relatively inexpensive in Canada, companies do not have the same motivation to reduce their reliance on energy here as in Japan. In fact, its energy resources make Canada an attractive location for energy-intensive industries. Moreover, Canada's climate and geography require Canadians to consume more energy in their daily business than residents of warmer regions with more concentrated populations.

Figure 2   Energy/GDP Ratios
(Toe/000s $1985 US)

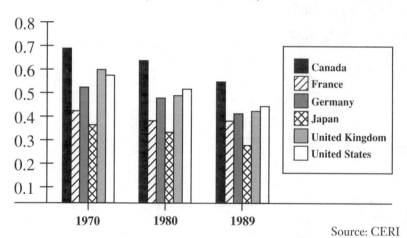

Source: CERI

Two developments which will affect energy policy in the industrialized countries in the years ahead are worth noting. The first is that the OECD countries, collectively, have lost the distinction of consuming more primary energy each year than all other countries.

This means that, increasingly, today's developing countries will be competing for energy commodities with today's industrialized countries. Second, as the developing countries become more developed and improve their living standards their E/GDP ratios will increase significantly. And, as the world outside the OECD becomes the world's largest energy consumer, that portion of the world will become the world's largest source of energy-related CO_2 emissions.

Figure 3   Shares of World Total Primary Energy Supply, 1989–2005

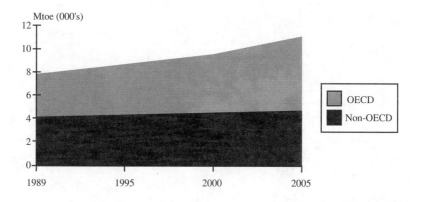

Figure 4   Energy-Related CO_2 Emissions (mtc)

	1973		1989		2005[a]	
	mtc	%	mtc	%	mtc	%
Non-OECD	1736	40	3102	53	5330	59
USSR	685	(39)	973	(31)	1454	(27)
Eastern Europe	331	(19)	420	(14)	590	(11)
China	273	(16)	664	(21)	1110	(21)
Asia-Pacific	166	(10)	419	(14)	933	(18)
Latin America	154	(9)	253	(8)	437	(8)
Middle East	47	(3)	169	(5)	502	(9)
Africa	80	(5)	190	(6)	304	(6)
OECD	2609	60	2793	47	3730	41
WORLD	4345	100	5895	100	9060	100

Source: IEA Secretariat

[a] Includes bunkers, petrochemical feedstocks and non-energy uses, which are excluded from the historical years.

Figure 5   The World Oil Price Outlook (WTI Crude; 1991 $US/b)

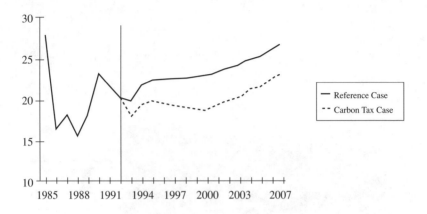

Sources: International Petroleum Encyclopaedia 1992; and (2) CERI (July 1992)

The Outlook for Oil

In the most recent CERI assessment of the outlook for the world oil market, the price of West Texas Intermediate crude oil moves slowly upwards, reaching $23 U.S. ($1991) per barrel by the year 2000 and $26 in 2006. (This translates into prices of about $21.50 and $24.50 for Brent crude in 2000 and 2006.) World oil demand in real terms is projected to increase at annual rates averaging under one percent, mainly because of sluggish gasoline demand and declining fuel oil demand, especially in the 1993–97 period. An increase in crude oil demand of about 9 MMb/d from 1992 to 2007 is seen as being readily accommodated by increased OPEC production. Total non-OPEC crude oil production falls slightly through the period and OPEC becomes the dominant supplier.

Other assumptions could lead to a quite different oil price forecast than that in the CERI reference case shown in Figure 5. For example, imposition of a carbon consumption tax would result in a reduction in the demand for oil which, if not partially or fully compensated for by cutbacks in OPEC production, would lower oil prices as illustrated. Another possibility with which OPEC might have to cope eventually is a marked increase in oil exports by the C.I.S.

Because there is more than sufficient oil to meet global demand through the next two decades, corporate planners will need to allow for the risk associated with possible downward movements in price. The more successful exploration and production companies will tend to be those which are more efficient at finding, developing and producing reserves. Marginal, high-cost oil producers do not have much to be optimistic about. In Canada, further development of Alberta's vast oil sands resource will be slow in coming unless there are more improvements in capital and operating costs. Canadian production of conventional light/medium crude oil is expected to continue to decline and Canada will become more and more dependent on foreign sources of light/medium crude. while exporting increasing volumes of heavy crude oil to the United States.

Natural Gas

In the wake of natural gas market deregulation, significant excess capacity to deliver gas has been apparent in Canada. As Figure 6 illustrates, this has depressed gas prices.

Figure 6 Alberta Average vs. US Gas Spot Wellhead Prices ($US/Mcf)

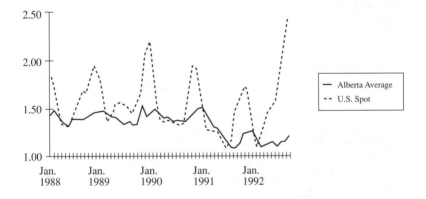

But growth in sales, especially Canadian gas exports, has brought demand for Canadian gas and the capacity to produce more in line and gas prices have begun to strengthen.

CERI recently completed a major study of the long-term outlook for world gas trade. The forecast of world region wellhead prices for gas contained in the study is shown in Figure 7.

One thing which North American and Western Europe share are the highest gas prices, on average, of the various world regions. As Figure 7 indicates, this is not expected to change.

Figure 7 World Wellhead Gas Prices (US $1991/Mcf)

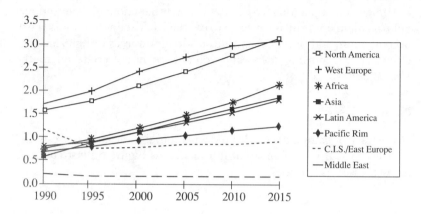

Globally, the real price of natural gas at the wellhead is projected to increase by about one percent per year to 2015. In North America and Western Europe the rate of increase is expected to be higher – in the vicinity of 2.5 percent per year – than in the Middle East and the C.I.S. which have enormous gas supply potentials.

Natural gas prices will be sufficiently high to encourage development and production of conventional reserves in all regions. As a consequence, world production of gas is expected to nearly double over the forecast period.

Figure 8 World Natural Gas Production (Tcf)

	1990	2015	Volume Increases	% Changes
North America	21.3	24.5	3.2	15
C.I.S./East Europe	26.8	49.5	22.7	85
Western Europe	6.5	7.3	0.8	12
Pacific Rim	3.6	8.5	4.9	136
Latin America	3.0	9.8	6.8	227
Africa	2.5	7.5	5.0	200
Middle East	3.2	15.7	12.5	391
Asia	1.6	9.7	8.1	506
Total	68.5	132.5	64.0	93

Because of the high cost of transporting natural gas, especially in liquified form, it will continue to be traded mainly on a regional rather than on a global basis.

As Figure 9 illustrates, international gas trade may almost triple from 1990 to 2015. But LNG's share of the total is not expected to increase. Essentially, this is because the cost of new grass root LNG facilities is generally such that LNG cannot compete with pipeline gas. For this reason, most of the incremental LNG facilities built during the period will be built to serve markets which have no or only limited access to pipeline gas, like Japan. In North America, where most of the available gas supply is or can be connected to markets by pipeline, potential new LNG supply sources effectively place a ceiling on the price in the vicinity of U.S. $4/m.c.f. (1991 dollars).

Figure 9   World Gas Trade (Tcf)

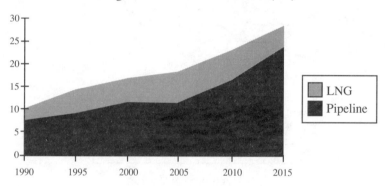

Coal

As Figure 10 illustrates, the world's proved recoverable reserves of coal are considerably greater than its combined oil and natural gas reserves. Western Europe holds about 10 percent of world coal reserves; North America, about 25 percent.

Figure 10   World Fossil Energy
Proved Recoverable Reserves, 1990 (Btoe)

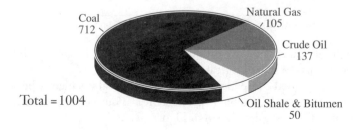

Canada has in the vicinity of 6.5 billion tons of proved recoverable reserves of coal. While these represent less than 1 percent of world reserves, they constitute close to 100 years' supply – a much greater R/P ratio than for Canadian oil or natural gas.

In 1990, Canadian coal production of 68 million tons was only 1.5 percent of world production. But Canada exported 31 million tons of coal – representing about 8.5 percent of world coal exports.

Figure 11   Canadian Production, Consumption and Exports of Coal

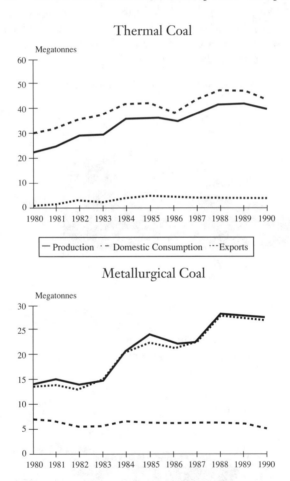

Growth of Canadian coal production since 1980 is largely due to increased exports of metallurgical coal.

Coal has remained competitive with oil and natural gas mainly because of tremendous gains in labour productivity. The Western Canadian experience in this regard is shown in Figure 12.

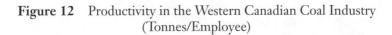

Figure 12 Productivity in the Western Canadian Coal Industry
(Tonnes/Employee)

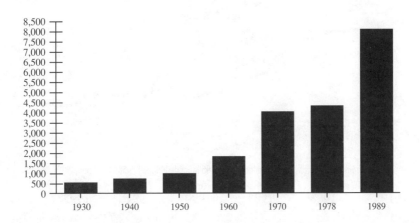

Competition among the coal-exporting countries scene is severe. Most Canadian coal exporters must cope with high transportation costs just to get to tidewater. And given union demands for higher pay rates and more stringent environmental regulations affecting coal combustion the outlook for Canada's coal industry is not particularly encouraging.

There are, nonetheless, grounds for optimism. Given the world's vast coal reserves, and likely further gains in coal production efficiencies, the price of coal is unlikely to increase as rapidly as the price of natural gas or oil. And new technologies will significantly reduce atmospheric emissions from coal combustion. These factors and the developing countries' needs for coal for power generation and for steel making suggest that demand for thermal and met. coal will continue to grow.

Uranium

Canada has some of the lowest cost, highest grade uranium ore reserves in the world and, as with natural gas and coal, is a net exporter.

The largest Canadian consumer of uranium fuel, by far, is Ontario Hydro. That utility's requirements have been increasing with the addition of four new reactors to its power generation system, at Darlington. However, some of its older nuclear plants have been out of service recently because of technical problems.

The U.S. dollar price of uranium oxide has trended downward since reaching a mid-1983 high of $24+ per lb. As shown in Figure 13, the spot price of U_3O_8 has been below U.S. $10.00 per pound for most of the last two years.

Figure 13   Uranium (U₃O₈) Spot Prices ($US/lb.)

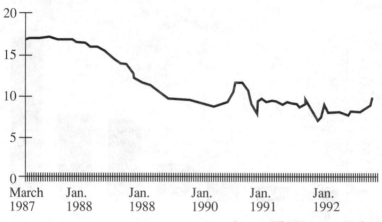

Source: The Uranium Exchange

Plans for many new nuclear plants were shelved in the aftermath of the Chernobyl and Three Mile Island incidents. In addition, slower-than-expected growth in electricity demand because of the recession and increased utility emphasis on slowing demand growth have reduced requirements for incremental generation capacity. These factors and government policy suggest that North Americans will see the nuclear power share of total electric power generation decline until well into the next century.

New nuclear power plants are being built elsewhere in the world and analysis of the outlook for uranium supply and demand suggests that the price will recover somewhat – probably to the $15 to $18 range. In large part the recovery will result from agreement by the C.I.S. not to dump uranium on the world market. Because the re-processing of 'spent' fuel will become economic if the price reaches the vicinity of $20.00, there is an effective ceiling on the price at about that level. In short, the health of the uranium mining industry will improve somewhat from the malady of recent years. However, investment is not without risk and the upside potential is limited.

Security of Supply

Canada and the United States have sufficient natural gas, coal and uranium to meet their requirements well into the next century. With oil the situation is different.

The United States imports about half of the crude oil which it consumes. If prolonged or frequent disruptions in the supply of Middle

Figure 14 Selected Energy and Environmental Data (1990 data)

	Canada	United Kingdom
% Total OECD TPES:	4.91	5.15
% Total OECD TPES:	2.58	2.70
Per capita TPES (toe per person):	7.60	3.70
TPES/GDP ratio (toe per US$1 000 1985):	0.50	0.40
Energy-related CO_2 emissions per capita (t CO_2 per person)	16.35	10.26
Energy-related CO_2 emissions per unit of GDP (t CO_2 per US$1 000 1985)	1.08	1.11
% Total energy-related OECD CO_2 emissions:	4.18	5.66
% Total energy-related World CO_2 emissions:	2.02	2.73

Source: The I.E.A.

East crude were perceived likely, the United States Government would undoubtedly undertake to ensure that the supply of oil needed for strategic defence purposes and to protect the U.S. economy from serious disruption is secure. But dissolution of the USSR and the disarming of Iraq have brought a considerable degree of political stability to the world, if not to Iraq and Russia. Consequently, the United States will probably not focus as seriously as otherwise on measures to reduce America's vulnerability to oil supply disruptions. The new administration will be more inclined to accelerate conversion to 'clean' transportation fuels. This will reduce crude oil demand and America's dependence on oil imports and increase consumption of natural gas.

In Canada oil imports will increase but the dependence on foreign crude is not nearly so great as in the U.S. There are no political or economic pressures for Canadians to be concerned about security of supply.

In the North American context, security of supply is also of concern to U.S. buyers of natural gas. However, the proportionality clause in the Canada/U.S. Free Trade Agreement protects U.S. buyers of Canadian gas. It guarantees them a share of the supply that *is* available in the event of a shortage which is proportional to the share of Canadian gas production which they have been buying.

Conclusion

These perspectives on the outlook for energy-commodity-producing industries have been prepared as background material for discussion. My view is that prospects for oil, coal and uranium prices are not very encouraging from the perspective of investors interested in coal or uranium production – at least not in North America. The outlook for higher natural gas prices makes investment in gas exploration, development and production attractive relative to oil, coal and uranium. Compared with other non-renewable fuels, natural gas sales will probably increase more rapidly in both Canada and the U.S. through the coming decade.

2 Supply and Demand Situations of Energy Industries

II A United Kingdom Perspective

Malcolm Wesley

Introduction

The United Kingdom, like Canada, is blessed with substantial fossil fuel reserves. Current estimate of proved reserves to production ratios are of the order of 300 years for coal, 6 years for oil and 12 years for natural gas. If probable and possible oil and gas reserves are included these ratios increase by about threefold. All of these fossil fuels (and uranium) are traded on a world-wide basis and are thus available to the UK as imports. World reserves of these fuels are plentiful; 238 years for coal, 43 years for oil and 58 years for gas. If probable, possible and unconventional reserves are included the ratios increase beyond a meaningful level.

Thus the availability of fossil fuels *per se* is not the critical issue in determining the supply and demand balance in the UK. Instead the balance of supply and demand and the mix of fuels are and will continue to be determined by economics, environmental and social concerns and the need for security of energy supplies. The aim is to meet the energy needs of the nation at the lowest possible cost in a timely and reliable manner whilst meeting environmental and social objectives.

This short note provides a UK perspective on these issues. It is written at a time when the UK government has just announced a wide ranging review of energy policy. Also the organization and structure of the UK energy industries over the past 6 years has gone through a radical transformation which has not yet bedded down. Moreover the continuing fiscal, political and commercial integration of the UK within Europe is in a state of flux. All these developments add to the uncertainty of how energy and demand issues will be resolved.

Energy demand

The traditional factors that affect energy demand and the mix of fuels supplying this demand are economic growth and energy prices. More recently environmental issues have also become an important factor that might dampen the growth in total energy requirements.

Total consumption of energy in the UK has declined in the last decade as energy intensity has fallen because of economic restructuring and price driven energy conservation. Over the next decade most forecasters see only a small growth in the total energy requirements of the country. A consensus view is that total primary energy requirements might grow by about 10% by the year 2000. Concerns over the environment make this prediction uncertain. The introduction of such concepts as a carbon tax and least cost planning (integrated resource planning or demand side management) remains a possibility.

Fuel switching away from coal and oil which are less environmentally friendly fuels towards natural gas is likely to occur. In particular there has been an upsurge in the use of natural gas for electricity generation, driven in part by environmental factors but also by pricing and the opening up of competitive generation. If this development persists it is expected that natural gas will increase its share of primary energy requirements from about 25% in 1990 to 37% by 2000.

The other potential for significant fuel switching is in the transportation sector. This market for natural gas is embyonic in the UK. The ground rules for establishing the economics of natural gas as a transportation fuel have recently been set through the level of taxation to be applied in the retail market. Technology is developing rapidly to meet the market needs. However, the impact on the energy mix is likely to be minimal over the next few years.

Energy supply

The public disaffection with nuclear power, and the slow progress being made in the introduction of renewable sources of energy means that the contribution to energy supply from these sources over the next decade is unlikely to grow significantly and fossil fuels will remain the major source of supply.

As stated earlier, there is an abundance of fossil fuels on a world-wide basis. The UK has substantial reserves of indigenous fuels, particularly of coal, although these reserves should perhaps be discounted to some extent because of coal's relative unattractiveness from an environmental point of view. Despite the indigenous reserves of fossil fuels in the UK, the country has been an importer of energy in the past and is likely to become increasingly so in the future. The imported/indigenous supply mix and the mix of fuels will be a function of economics, environmental and social concerns and the need to have an adequate level of security.

To a large extent the economic issues have been left to market forces. This has resulted in the importation of all three fossil fuels to some extent and a switch away from oil and coal towards natural gas. Environmental concerns have supported this switch in fuels. As indigenous supplies of oil and natural gas deplete and the cost of supply rises there will be an increasing trend to imported supplies. This is likely to be relatively modest over the next decade but thereafter will become more significant and cause energy security to become more important.

The energy security issue as well as social and environmental concerns are not necessarily reflected in market force mechanisms. Taxation, subsidization and direct government intervention are tools available to adjust the mechanism to meet policy objectives.

From an energy security perspective the UK is reasonably placed not only because of its indigenous supplies of coal but also because it is geographically well placed in relation to the vast reserves of natural gas in the CIS, North Africa and the Middle East. It is only a matter of time before the UK natural gas system becomes physically integrated with the rest of Europe. The importation of LNG provides an alternative route to access global supplies of natural gas. The integration of Europe is likely to result in the energy security issue being addressed on a European scale. A combination of incentives to continue the development of indigenous supplies, the diversification of geographical source and fuel mix and strategic storage will all be used to achieve an adequate level of supply security.

The social consequence of increasing the importation of fuels and the switch to natural gas from indigenous coal has been and remains a thorny problem. This issue set in the context of broader energy policy for the UK is the subject of study at present.

The key components of cost in the energy supply chain are production, delivery to the market, taxation and investors' profit. Taxation is the tool available to governments to extract any economic rent between the cost of supply and the competitive price of the market. Although there is an abundant resource of fossil fuels governments must ensure that they use taxation wisely to ensure an equitable balance between producing countries, investors and customers' interests if the resources are to be developed in a timely manner.

Conclusions

Demand for energy in the UK will grow slowly over the next decade. A carbon tax or the adoption of least cost planning concepts have the potential to slow this growth. The mix of fuels will change to favour natural gas at the expense of coal and possibly oil. This change will be driven by environmental concerns and economics but may be limited to some extent by social concerns.

The use of natural gas for electricity generation will be a major driver in the switch of fuels. Natural gas for transportation is unlikely to emerge as a significant market in this timescale.

Market forces will be the major determinant in the supply of energy both in terms of fuel mix and in the balance of imported versus indigenous supplies. The nuclear and renewable energy components of supply are unlikely to grow significantly over the next ten years. Security of supply will remain an issue but the UK is relatively well placed to access imported supplies. Measures to ensure security of supply are likely to be coordinated on a European basis.

Market forces alone will not necessarily ensure that energy security, environmental and social objectives will be met. Government direction to achieve the objectives will be necessary to supplement market force mechanisms.

There is an abundant world-wide supply of fossil fuels and a well-developed delivery infrastructure. Governments will have to ensure that producer countries, investors and customer interests are treated equally equitably if supplies are to be developed in a timely manner and the supply infrastructure maintained and expanded to meet market demands.

3 Alternative Energy Sources

I Canadian Situations

Michael R. Robertson

SUMMARY

Forecasting energy supply and demand is an uncertain science. However, one certainty is that there will always be a requirement for capital investment in energy projects. In the coming decades, environmental factors will strongly influence these investments by the way energy is:

– used (increased efficiency);
– produced (reduced toxic emissions);
– marketed (real versus perceived environmental impacts).

Declining Canadian conventional petroleum reserves will change the mix of domestic crudes as Canada moves towards more synthetic crude and heavy sour oil. This change will require capital investment in refineries. Alternate fuels will increasingly move to fill specialty markets. There are no signs at present of a rush to replace Canada's oil infrastructure with alternates until new energy sources are proven safe and economical. Natural gas, however, is well-positioned to continue to steadily gain market share. If another oil price shock occurs, the switch to natural gas could occur even more rapidly.

Technology will be the wild card of the future. A breakthrough in any of the alternate fuels technologies could cause the use of crude oil based energy sources to decline more rapidly.

Governments may also move to influence the energy supply mix through economic instruments, support of research, efficiency programs and through their own buying decisions.

CANADA'S CURRENT ENERGY SUPPLY AND DEMAND MIX

Canada is a large country with a cold climate, and an economy which is based on its considerable natural resources. On a per capita basis, Canada is the highest producer[1] of uranium, nickel, copper, potash, gypsum, zinc, barley and newsprint.

Energy in Canada is used intensively, largely because of our geography and economy. Canada is primarily dependent on oil and gas, which account for over 70% of energy supply. This dependency will continue for a considerable time.

Figure 1   Canada's Domestic Energy Availability 1991

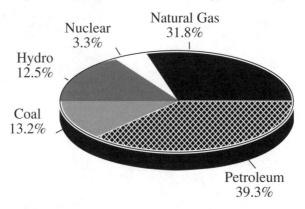

Nuclear
3.3%

Natural Gas
31.8%

Hydro
12.5%

Coal
13.2%

Petroleum
39.3%

Source: Stats Canada 57-003

Presently available domestic supplies come from nuclear and hydro power, oil and gas and coal (Figure 1). Canada is a net exporter of natural gas and electricity and to a small extent of oil. Electricity generated by burning coal, oil or natural gas is not counted as primary energy.

Canada relies on oil and gas in all sectors of its economy (Figure 2). For example, the only practical option for transportation currently is refined petroleum products and natural gas. No single approach that stimulates demand for alternative energy appears ready to change Canada's overall energy demand patterns. Current market diversity suggests that the use of alternate fuels will take many years to penetrate Canadian markets. In order to successfully increase the use of alternate fuels, programs will need to be tailored to individual economic sectors and subsectors.

Figure 2   Energy Demand in Canada (by sector) 1991

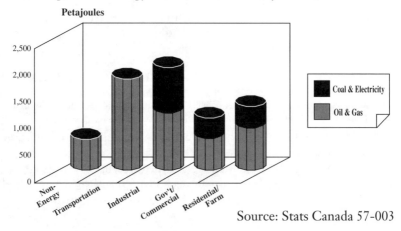

Source: Stats Canada 57-003

Canada's transportation network is heavily oriented towards the personal vehicle. Governments continue to spend heavily to reinforce this vehicular orientation. For example, it is anticipated[2] that $14 billion will be spent over ten years by the federal government in upgrading Canada's 24,500 kilometre national highway system (less than three percent of our total road network). Even more will be spent if the bridge from New Brunswick to Prince Edward Island is approved.

Canadians currently choose overwhelmingly in favour of driving to work (Figure 3). The number of road vehicles is also increasing, yet the consumption of gasoline is declining slightly. One result has been increasing rationalization of refinery capacity within Canada because of over supply.

Figure 3   Personal Choice for Travel to Work

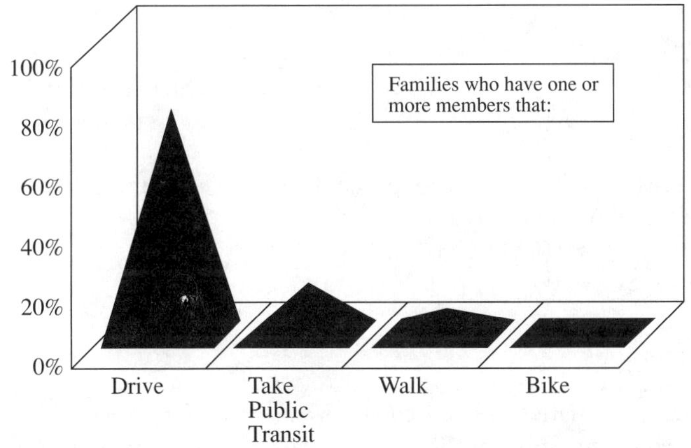

SOURCE: Stats Canada, Spring 1992
Canadian Social Trends

Electrical energy has a much more diverse infrastructure in Canada. Power sources include:

– nuclear, coal, oil and gas fired steam generation power plants;
– small-scale wind turbine farms;
– gas fired co-generation plants;
– hydro powered turbines;
– diesel engine powered generators.

ENVIRONMENTAL DRIVING FORCES

Canada has a number of environmental challenges including, from a fuels point of view, issues such as:

Figure 4   Electricity Generation Capacity (%)

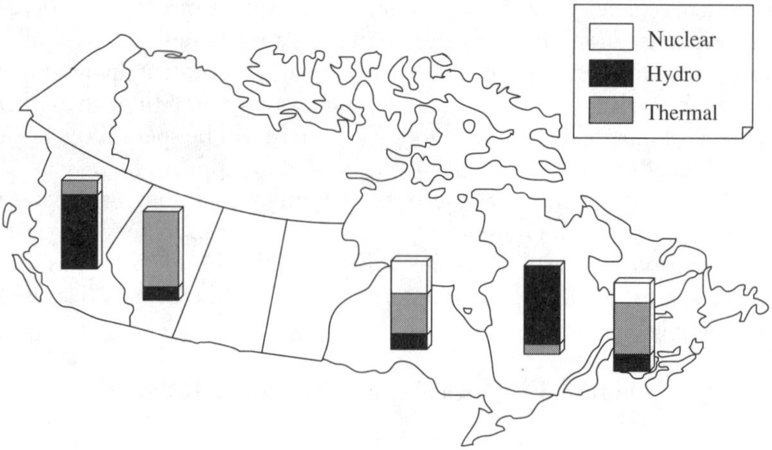

Source: CPA Statistics Handbook
Nameplate listings

- toxic emissions (benzene, lead, particulates, CO and others)
- ground level ozone (NO_X and VOC)
- greenhouse gases (CO_2, CH_4, CFCs)
- acid rain (SO_X and NO_X)

Toxic Emissions

Canada has an initiative called the *Priority Substances List* which is looking at the toxicity of a number of chemicals. Benzene, a component of gasoline, is one of the chemicals under consideration. Efforts to reduce benzene emissions could range from lower worker exposure limits to reduced benzene content of gasoline. Capital upgrading would be required to most Canadian refineries for the latter measure.

Lead emissions from gasolines have been eliminated in Canada since December, 1990, as refiners invested in equipment to make lead free gasolines. However, other issues remain. For example, Canada struggles with weighing the costs and benefits of using a manganese based octane enhancer, MMT (methylcyclopentadi-enylmanginese tricarbonyl).

A program to desulphurize on-road diesel is well on its way to help diesel engine makers meet targets of reducing particulate emissions. Diesel engine makers are also considering catalytic convertors and particulate traps as further refinements to reduce emissions. At the same time, engine makers are investigating the use of natural gas and methanol mixes in diesel engines to meet future emissions requirements.

Some gasoline marketers are adding chemicals to oxygenate gasoline on a small scale basis in order to reduce toxic emissions. MTBE (methyl tertiary butyl ether) is being added by one West Coast marketer, while another Western marketer is adding ethanol, made from grain, to gasoline.

Most new cars in Canada are equipped with catalytic convertors to reduce emissions of unburnt hydrocarbons (VOCs), NO_x (oxides of nitrogen) and CO (carbon monoxide). Catalyst poisoning by sulphur in gasoline is being explored by the U.S. Auto-Oil research program as a major quality factor influencing automobile emissions. The research program is intended to find the best reformulation for reducing toxic emissions and emissions causing ground level ozone.

Ground Level Ozone

A yellowish haze often occurs near large centres of people at ground level, commonly known as ground level ozone (O_3) or 'photochemical smog'. It is formed by a reaction of NO_x and VOCs (volatile organic compounds), in the presence of sunlight.

Canada has three major regions (Vancouver area, St. John and the corridor between Quebec City and Windsor) where ozone limits periodically exceed current Canadian human health standards. To reduce the risk of excessive exposure to ozone, a number of programs are outlined in Canada's NO_x/VOC management plan. Several initiatives are aimed at the composition of fuels and their distribution system.

Investments are being made to collect gasoline vapour from primary distribution terminals (Stage I) in the Vancouver and Toronto areas. It is expected that Stage I will be extended to other problem areas in Canada. Secondary vapour collection from retail sites (Stage II) in sensitive areas is expected to be regulated within the next ten years.[3] Gasoline volatility is also being reduced during summer months by lowering the vapour pressure of gasoline (currently 72 kPa in the Vancouver area). Since the primary means of achieving lower vapour pressure is to remove butane from the gasoline, a butane over supply problem is created.

Greenhouse Gases

A layer of gases in the outer region of the atmosphere traps the sun's heat and makes our planet hospitable to life. Research indicates that man's activities have caused an increasing amount of greenhouse gases to accumulate in the atmosphere. Many scientific authorities suggest that these gases will lead to an increase in the average temperature of the atmosphere (global warming).

Facing the Energy Challenge

Figure 5 CO_2 equivalency of greenhouse gases.

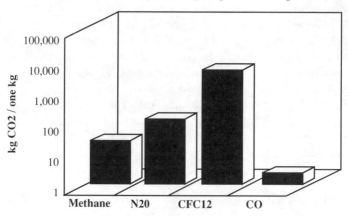

Source: Boyle & Ardill
The Greeenhouse Effect

Different types of greenhouse gases have differing potentials to trap heat (forcing factors). While not the most potent gas, CO_2 (carbon dioxide) is the most common and all others are often, compared to it (Figure 5). Principal greenhouse gases emitted by oil and natural gas consumption are CO_2 and CH_4 (methane) with some N_2O (nitrous oxide). CH_4 and N_2O have a significantly higher forcing factor than CO_2. Therefore, when a choice is made to reduce greenhouse gases, the selection process must take into account emissions of all types.

Generally, the heavier a hydrocarbon, the higher the emissions of CO_2 are per unit of energy released (Figure 6).

Figure 6 CO_2 emissions by fuel type.

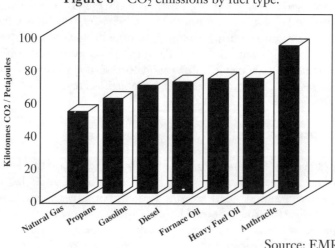

Source: EMR 1989

Some researchers have calculated that a leakage rate of over five percent CH_4, from natural gas systems, offsets the CO_2 emissions saved from burning natural gas instead of coal.

Acid Rain

Gaseous emissions of SO_X (sulphur dioxide) and NO_X are converted in the atmosphere to sulphuric and nitric acids. When these acids fall to earth as rain they can damage[4] streams, lakes, groundwater, arable land, forest and buildings.

The main sources of SO_X emissions are coal fired electricity generation stations and non-ferrous smelters. Vehicle emissions and other fuel combustion types are the main sources of NO_X. While not all regions of Canada are sensitive to acid rain, 80% of Canadians live in areas that are.

In Ontario, four companies are the source of over 80% of SO_X emissions (1980 levels). Ontario Hydro[5] is the second largest emitter. Canada has been working to reduce acid rain with a number of programs. The latest step was a long range pollution treaty with the United States.

The emphasis on reducing SO_X emissions has caused petroleum refiners to reduce the sulphur content in their heavy fuel oils. Sometimes called Bunker C, these heavy fuels are sold primarily to power or steam generation plants and for ship boilers. Domestic heavy fuel oils are now in the range of 1.5% to 2.0% weight percent sulphur. Without facility upgrading, Canadian refiners will use expensive sweet crude in place of cheaper heavy or sour crudes to make heavy fuel oil.

DOMESTIC SUPPLY OF CRUDE OIL AND GAS

Most of Canada's deliverable reserves of crude oil and gas are found in Western Canada, with some volumes in the environmentally sensitive Arctic regions. Canada's sizeable East Coast reserves will not enter continuous production until 1997. There is presently little infrastructure to deliver domestic frontier crudes to market.

Crude Oil

Canada has a network of pipelines to deliver light, heavy and synthetic crudes to refineries west of Quebec. Recently the pipeline extension from Ontario to Quebec was closed because volumes being shipped were too small to be economical. Quebec and the Maritimes will be reliant on offshore crudes until the east coast Hibernia project starts to deliver crude in 1997.

Figure 7   Crude supply and refining network

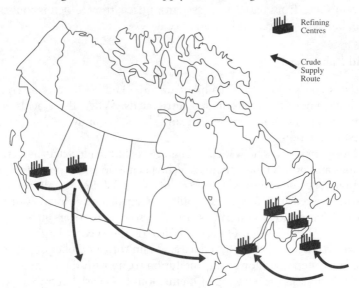

Natural Gas

Canada had 2.8 trillion cubic metres of natural gas reserves at the end of
1990. This represents 2.3% of the world's reserves and a supply life of 28
years based on current production. In addition to meeting its own needs,
Canada exports a significant amount of domestic oil and gas production
to the United States, through a rapidly growing pipeline network.

Figure 8   Canadian reserves of crude oil.

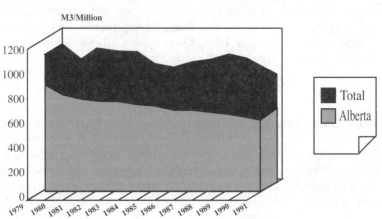

Source: CPA Statistical Handbook, 1991

Western Canada Sedimentary Basin

Alberta's conventional light crude reserves are forecast to decline by 50% between 1988[6] and 2003. As reserves decline, heavy and synthetic crudes will become a larger part of the crude mix. Synthetics must be mixed with other crudes to run in a conventional refinery. Alberta has two specialty refineries that can process 100% synthetic crude.

Heavy Crude Oil

The market for heavy oil has been poor because of the high sulphur content and high yields of low value products. Investment in upgrading and sulphur removal is required before demand for heavy crudes increases, such as the upgrader currently being built in Lloydminster on the Alberta-Saskatchewan border. A short-term alternative is to export lower priced heavy oil and import expensive sweet crude.

Sour Light Crude Oil

As sulphur specifications for refined product become more stringent, refiners will have to commit to more capital spending in order to process light sour oil. Again, the short-term alternative is to run expensive light sweet crude.

Synthetic Crude Oil

The Athabasca tar sands have reserves of 32 billion cubic metres that can be retrieved with present technology. Total reserves are estimated at 150 to 450 billion cubic metres. Without the two commercial plants currently producing synthetic crude from the tar sands, Canada would be a net importer of crude.

Heavy power demands at the mining and upgrading stage of synthetic oil production result in more $CO_2/SO_x/NO_x$ per unit of energy produced than conventional light oil. There are also some long-term treatment questions about the waste water created during the mining and separation processes.

Since the late 1970s, capital investment in one of the commercial plants, Syncrude, has been about \$4.5 billion dollars. The plant has recently produced its 63 millionth cubic metre.

WHAT ALTERNATIVES ARE AVAILABLE?

It is not always clear what is meant by the term 'alternate energy source'. For instance, in Saskatchewan, nuclear energy is currently an alternative under discussion with regard to fossil fuels. In Ontario, there is a moratorium on nuclear energy, and co-generation using natural gas is an alternative increasingly discussed.

Home heating in Western Canada is almost completely powered by natural gas but in the Maritimes there remains a high reliance on furnace oil or wood.

Easy Gains

Even when there are clear operating cost and environmental benefits to switching energy supply, infrastructure can be a significant barrier. For example, until the natural gas pipeline system is extended to the Maritimes, it is unlikely there will be any large scale switch from furnace oil.

Sales of natural gas within Canada have risen nearly 28% from 1978 to 1990[7]. The quickest growth has been by the residential sector (45% over the same time period). Natural gas burns with less SO_x, particulates (soot) and CO_2 compared to wood or furnace oil.

Exports of natural gas to the United States have also risen by nearly 52% in the same period. Last year[8] saw a one year record jump in exports of 24%. A $3 billion pipeline expansion was recently completed into the northeastern U.S. Canadian natural gas can now be delivered across the breadth of the U.S. Americans have been encouraged to switch to lower sulphur content fuels by the recently passed U.S. Clean Air Act which, like Canada, has set specific caps for sulphur emissions.

Figure 9   Canadian natural gas sales.

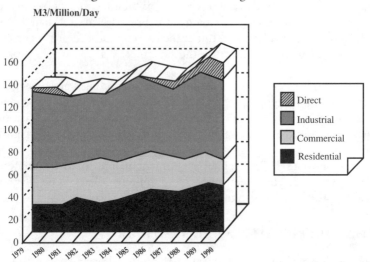

Source: CPA Statistical Handbook, 1991

Propane is one alternative fuel that can be readily used by automobiles today. Canada has some 5,000 stations capable of refuelling with propane, and many companies will economically convert conventional vehicles. However, even with propane's lower price, the conversion cost requires a number of years to pay back, and a large part of Canada's existing propane fleet is high mileage vehicles. When propane vehicles become available from the factory, the conversion cost barriers will decrease.

Natural gas for vehicles can also be used in Canada, although not with the same ease as propane. There are less than one hundred retail outlets and fewer conversion companies. Advances in the near future include factory availability of natural gas engines, fuel injection and home fuel compressors, allowing people to refuel their vehicles at home.

Difficult Choices

Where costs are higher and environmental benefits are not clear, switching to alternate energies will occur at a much slower rate unless driven by a government policy.

There are a number of transportation alternate fuels presently being reviewed. All have disadvantages as well as benefits. Because of infrastructure required and incomplete knowledge at present of environmental impacts of these fuels, growth is likely to be in limited markets or at only a slow and steady pace.

An example of government induced alternate fuel growth is the California Zero Emission Vehicle (ZEV) program. Starting in the year 1998, a minimum of two percent of the new car fleet is required to have zero emissions. Two other states have also adopted this goal. Most car companies are working on electric vehicles to meet this market demand.

The Canadian federal government's Green Plan includes a policy to support the use of alternate fuels:

> Initiatives in this area will include accelerated development and market penetration of alternative transportation fuels, including expansion of natural gas markets, increased availability of alternative fuel vehicles, and encouragement of ethanol and methanol as automotive fuels and fuel feedstocks, and support for research and development of alternative fuel sources such as hydrogen.
>
> The Green Plan, 1990

The Refiners' Challenge

The sulphur balance in refineries will become increasingly complex. As the crude supply average sulphur content increases and refined products' sulphur content is lowered, refinery emissions of SO_x must be maintained or reduced.

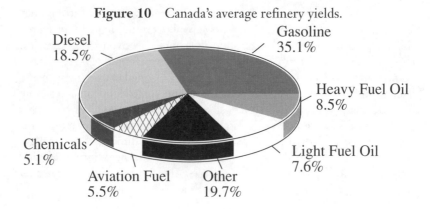

Figure 10   Canada's average refinery yields.

Source: CPA Statistics Handbook

The mix of refined products produced in Canada shows the challenges that refiners face. It is likely that heavy fuel oil and furnace oil will continue to decline in importance because of competing natural gases. Other uses (e.g. lubricating oils and asphalts), aviation fuels and chemical feedstock demands are likely to remain constant as there is no readily apparent substitute. Gasoline and diesel fuels, primarily used in transportation, face the greatest uncertainty. Even if the alternative fuels make no in-roads, there will be pressure to change the composition of these traditional fuels to reduce their environmental impact.

These challenges will require capital investments in Canadian refineries to meet the new product mixes and crude mixes. Rationalization of the refinery network is the first step in meeting these demands.

Case Study: Vancouver Island

As alternative energy sources become feasible or cost competitive, they will erode existing markets. In 1991, a natural gas pipeline was laid from the mainland to Vancouver Island. The project cost approximately $340 million and has some 534 kilometres of pipeline. An additional $25 million dollars is being spent helping home owners convert from home heating oil, electricity and wood to natural gas. Heavy fuel oil at pulp and paper plants will also be displaced.

In addition to the environmental benefits associated with switching to natural gas, it is anticipated that the risk of product spill from tankers will be reduced. Most petroleum products are presently shipped by barge or ship from the mainland.

Hydrogen

Hydrogen is the fuel of the future and always will be...

Anonymous

Today many researchers are trying to change this preconception about hydrogen as a fuel. Although there are no emissions other than water vapour from burning hydrogen, it has a low energy density by volume. Hydrogen is thus very difficult to store, particularly for vehicle applications. These difficulties have kept commercial development at a standstill.

Mazda is adapting its rotary engine for hydrogen. It believes that its technology will be a key to entering the ZEV market in the United States. A Canadian development is the Ballard hydrogen-polymer fuel cell, which uses hydrogen to generate electricity. Its first commercial application will be to power a Vancouver public bus in 1992.

The Ballard fuel cell's advantage is that it has four times the power density as previous fuel cell technologies.

ELECTRIC POWER

Canada's domestic electric power consumption increased by 46% during the 1980s. As the economy grows, it is anticipated that power demand will also grow. Utilities will be faced with the challenge of meeting this growth without exceeding emissions constraints.

Canadian utilities are a mixed group of government owned and privately owned companies. Generally, they have a monopoly over a given province, however, there are some regional power companies. For example, in Alberta, TransAlta Utilities, a private company, provides electricity to all of the province except for the cities of Edmonton and Medicine Hat, which have municipally owned power companies.

Nearly all Canadian utilities have adopted an 'efficiency and conservation' ethic to help reduce anticipated increased demand. Other strategies include purchasing power from independent producers. This has opened the door for many alternative energy projects.

Nuclear Energy

Nuclear energy in Canada is a relatively small source of energy (3.3% of total energy availability). All of Canada's capacity is in Ontario, Quebec and New Brunswick. Ontario, the largest user of nuclear power, has declared a nuclear development moratorium. Despite the moratorium, Ontario currently has excess power generation capacity and private producers are building small scale plants that continue to increase that capacity. The City of Kingston is planning to drop out of the Ontario Hydro system by building its own natural gas fired turbine generator.[10]

The benefits are annual savings of $10 to $15 million and environmentally clean power. A natural gas fired co-generation plant is planned near the City of Windsor that will supply power and steam to local heavy industries.

Only two provinces are currently considering nuclear power, Saskatchewan and New Brunswick. Current nuclear technology power plants, e.g. CANDU reactors, take about seven years to build.

We are unlikely to see any growth in available nuclear power prior to the year 1999 and very small growth in the following years to 2005.

Figure 11   Electrical power generation costs (cost ¢/kwh)

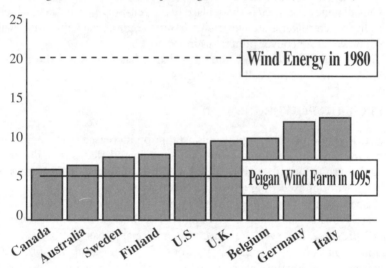

Source: Financial Post

Other Alternatives

A barrier to the expansion of alternate power is the cost of generation. Electricity from an Alberta coal fired power plant is in the order of 2.5 cents per kilowatt hour (¢/kwh). Power from a small project of wind turbines (wind farm) scheduled to come online in 1995, in Alberta, will cost 5.2¢/kwh. This cost is remarkable because in the early 1980s the cost was about 20¢/kwh. Advances in turbine design have resulted in a dramatic reduction in cost.

Solar technology also has undergone similar technological advances. Even so, it is still only cost effective for low power applications in regions that are not fed from an existing electrical distribution grid.

With some of the world's lowest electric power costs, Canada's utilities are understandably reluctant to use solar and wind technology on any large scale. Ontario, with one of Canada's highest electrical rates, is under pressure to use natural gas co-generation to help lower costs.

Hydrogen fuel cells have been discussed for small scale power generation use in Canada. Some of the first commercial uses of fuel cells for power generation have occurred in California.

INVESTMENT IN THE FUTURE

Oil companies must continually make heavy capital investment in exploration, production, refineries, terminals, bulk plants and service stations. All these facilities are facing complex environmental changes requiring capital investment. Capital needs for existing technology will compete against new ventures to produce alternate fuels.

Examples of capital requirements:

NGV compressor stations	$250,000 to $400,000
NGV home compressors	$3,000/per home
Propane vehicle stations	$50,000
680 megawatt Candu reactor	$600 million
World scale MTBE plant	$300 million
Diesel desulphurizing unit	$80 million
Heavy oil upgrader	$1.6 billion
Hibernia east coast oil	$5.2 billion

CONCLUSION

Continued reliance on fossil fuels

Canada is becoming increasingly dependent on imported oil in eastern and central Canada. With a heavy dependency on personal vehicles, we will be sensitive to any oil price shocks.

Responses to past price shocks have been to increase the use of Canada's own crudes to insulate its economy. In the future, this strategy would require heavy capital investments in frontier or synthetic oil production. Either source of oil has some environmental challenges. The alternative to frontier crudes or synthetic oil usage may be an increasing investment in the natural gas infrastructure. With its environmental benefits and our abundant domestic supplies, the alternative looks very favourable. This switch would make a permanent shift in Canada's energy demand patterns. We are already seeing a measurable movement towards increased use of natural gas across North America.

Electrical demand will steadily increase

The rate of increase in demand is expected to be abated by demand side management, using programs based on efficiency and conservation. One growth area may be with small scale power generators using natural gas co-generation units. Some small wind farms are also expected to be built in the next decade. Solar generation will likely remain an option for remote regions or standalone appliances like garden lights or Honda's new solar powered canoe.[11]

Technology shock could increase demand for an alternative

In the longer term, a technology shock (light weight, fast recharge and cheap batteries) could also drive our economy to invest in alternative energy. For example, a recent development on a battery charging plug sharply reduces charging time and makes charging safer for the operator.

If the hydrogen-polymer fuel cell, currently being developed on the West Coast, proves to be commercially viable, markets for diesel fuel could erode more quickly. The fuel cell has the potential to make a vehicle, like a city bus, emission free. The commercial diesel market has relatively few vehicles, which could be converted much more quickly than the personal vehicle market.

Increasing markets for natural gas

If neither a price nor a technology shock occurs, there will be a gradual erosion of traditional oil markets by alternative fuels. Specialty markets, like propane for medium duty trucks and natural gas for large commercial fleets, will develop as investment in vehicles takes place.

In the short term, a likely scenario appears to be one of natural gas eroding other conventional fuel sources. A long shot appears to be hydrogen fuel cells replacing batteries in electric cars.

Continued focus on environmental issues

No matter what direction the energy industry takes over the next decade, environmental concerns will play an important role. However, it is critical that we improve our ability to correctly measure the environmental impact of various energy options, so proper decisions can be made in encouraging the use of different alternatives.

Environmental improvement in conventional energy supply

Several of the currently identified environmental issues associated with carbon based fuels are the subject of substantial improvement through technological development, both on the fuel side, and in the combustion unit. Fuel composition and distribution will continue to change, particularly in refined oil products, to address major issues such as ground level ozone, particulates, and carbon monoxide exceedances in cities. A true 'wild card' in the debate, however, will be the rate at which governments move to implement the 1992 Convention on Climate Change; either through imposition of such measures as carbon taxes, or with other economic incentives which might accelerate any fuel shifting towards non-carbon based energy sources, such as hydro or nuclear produced electricity. A likely time frame for such intervention, however, is only in the 10–15 year framework.

REFERENCES

1. *Canada and Global Warming*, Federal Government publication, 1992.
2. *Macleans Magazine*, October 5, 1992.
3. *Environmental Code of Practice for Vapour Recovery in Gasoline Distribution Networks*, Canadian Council of Environmental Ministers, March 1991.
4. *Planet Under Stress*, Mungall and McLaren–Editors for the Royal Society of Canada, 1990.
5. *Stopping Acid Rain*, Government of Canada publication, undated.
6. 'Deadline: 2011', A. Boras, *Calgary Herald*, September 24, 1992.
7. *CPA Statistical Handbook*, CPA, 1991.
8. 'Gas Sales: Up, Up and Away', G. Jaremko, *Calgary Herald*, September 25, 1992.
9. 'Island Faces Higher Natural Gas Prices', *The Vancouver Sun*, June 4, 1991.
10. 'Kingston Expects To Save Millions By Generating Its Own Electrical Power', T. Spears, *The Ottawa Citizen*, September 16, 1992.
11. 'Fairweather Friend', *Globe and Mail*, October 6, 1992.

3 *Alternative Energy Sources*

II Energy Mix and Alternative Energy in the UK:
A Sustainability Perspective

Roger Levett

INTRODUCTION
Perspective

'Energy *perspectives*' is a particularly helpful conference subtitle for this paper. The point about perspective is that how things look depends on where you stand. If you stand in the middle of downtown Vancouver, your view is dominated by the few buildings near you, with more distant ones appearing very small. If instead you look in across the water from North Vancouver they all appear at more or less the same scale; however many are completely hidden by the ones in front.

People within the energy industries will naturally ask 'how must my industry, or company, respond to environmental pressures'. The industry as it is will be the starting point, the environment another external problem which needs to be responded to like labour costs or market uncertainties. The brief I have been given – to cover the changing energy mix, the prospects for alternative energy sources, and the impact of environmental concerns on energy supply and consumption – reflects this viewpoint.

However from the viewpoint of a specialist in sustainable development this list is back to front. It is necessary instead to start from the environmental realities, and then see what consumption levels, supply mix and opportunities for alternative sources they dictate. Many elements of the picture this gives will already be familiar to people viewing from elsewhere. But the way they stand in relation to each other may be startlingly different. And what are dominant landmarks from one perspective may not be visible at all from another.

Structure of the paper

The first half of the paper indicates how the UK energy scene looks from the perspective of sustainability. It starts by explaining how that loaded and ambiguous term sustainable development can be understood (section 2) and applied to energy (section 3). This enables us to show why, contrary to common belief, environmental sustainability is not necessarily opposed to economic development. Section 4 offers a more subtle interpretation of the relationship between the two and deduces from it the kinds of energy development which are sustainable, and section 5 summarizes the prospects for these in the UK

The second half of the paper considers how UK policy and practice matches up to the demands of sustainability. Section 6 shows the limitations of the market from the energy consumption side. Section 7 recounts how the UK government's policies have applied these same limitations to much of the energy supply industry, and section 8 explains why, despite being an exception to much of this, nuclear power is no solution. Section 9 shows how the current problems of energy supply are simply the predictable consequence of the last decade's policies, and the concluding section 10 argues that a return to the old-fashioned idea that governments should have policies offers the best hope for sustainable energy in the UK.

WHAT DOES SUSTAINABLE DEVELOPMENT MEAN?

The length and obscurity of a lot of the terminology and documents about sustainable development might suggest it is a complex or difficult idea. In fact it is extremely simple and obvious. (This is not to say that implementing it is easy. This point is returned to at the end of the paper.)

Sustainability is based on the concept of 'intergenerational equity'. This is simply the seaside guest house admonition 'please leave this room as you would wish to find it' writ large: 'Please leave this planet as you would wish to find it.' One of the speakers at last year's Colloquium described it as 'behaving as if we want the planet to stay'.

Two classic formulations of sustainable development echo this: Chief Seattle's '*We do not inherit the world from our ancestors: we borrow it from our children*' and the Brundtland Commission's: '*Satisfying the needs of the present without reducing the ability of future generations to satisfy their own needs*'.

A principle of action like this cannot be 'proved', or deduced from facts about the world. The most you can say about anyone who does not share it is that you don't care for their morals. However most people generally behave in their personal affairs as if the future matters. They make sacrifices to educate their children; they plant trees that will not mature until after they die; they make bequests to third-world charities. One can argue that it is only consistent with this 'revealed preference' for people also to act so as to leave those children and trees a healthy environment to live in, and to avoid adding to the problems those charities try to address.

The second key concept of sustainability is 'Maintenance of the regenerative capacity of ecosystems'. This just means 'Don't kill the goose that lays the golden eggs'. The planet can give us an ample living provided we aren't too greedy, and don't consume so fast we erode the systems that provide it – in other words, don't breach ecological carrying capacity limits.

This third key concept can also be easily paraphrased. Since the words are Dickens' it is a bit more prolix than the first two, but it is still clear enough:

> Annual income twenty pounds, annual expenditure nineteen six, result happiness.
> Annual income twenty pounds, annual expenditure twenty nought and six, result misery.

SUSTAINABILITY AND ENERGY

The argument so far has been entirely abstract. It has practical signifi-cance because there is strong evidence that we *are* breaking some important carrying capacity limits; that we *are* undermining the world's ability to continue to support life; and that we *will* leave the earth in a far worse state than our successors would have wished to find it. The argument matters for energy policy because the single most important cause of our unsustainable impacts is our current pattern of energy generation and use.

The key issue is global warming. Burning fossil fuels releases carbon dioxide. Carbon dioxide in the atmosphere traps solar heat. (Methane, the main ingredient in natural gas and a by-product of some other energy operations, traps a great deal more, molecule for molecule). The more carbon dioxide there is in the atmosphere the more heat is retained. Carbon dioxide levels are rising sharply because human use of fossil fuels is adding it to the atmosphere at a rate that far outstrips the rate that natural systems can remove it again.

The interaction between atmosphere, oceans, evaporation, cloud cover, amount and distribution of rainfall, ground temperature, ice melt, crop belt movements and so on is immensely complex and far from fully understood. However the best climate models available predict massive disruption to agriculture, sea level rises that will inundate large areas of fertile and highly populated land, and an increase in destructive extreme weather. Such evidence as we have tends to support the models. For example the impact on weather of Mount Pinatubo's discharges into the upper atmosphere has been very close to what the models predict.

Uncertainty, risk and lead times

In the absence of conclusive scientific proof some politicians of a non-interventionist cast of mind still think we should wait and see whether global warming is for real before making sacrifices to avert it. This seems to me to ignore one crucial fact and to misunderstand the nature of risk.

The crucial fact is that there are long lead times: changes in human behaviour take decades to work through into the atmosphere. Even if we stopped using fuel tomorrow global warming would get worse for decades because of what we have already put into the atmosphere. If we wait for the evidence of damage to be irrefutable before we act at all, the further damage still in the pipeline may prove disastrous. We may indeed already be past this stage.

The point about risk is that there is more to it than just the ratio of likely benefits to possible costs. Suppose someone offered you a gamble where you had a nine-times-in-ten chance of winning ten times your stake and a one-in-ten chance of losing it. You would wager ten pounds on these terms without hesitation: winning a hundred pounds would be nice, losing ten irritating but nothing to lose sleep over. You might wager ten thousand pounds, although you would think carefully first and do it a lot less blithely. Winning a hundred thousand would be very nice; losing ten thousand pounds might not be a total disaster but it would be a serious setback to most people.

You would probably not accept exactly the same gamble if the stake was ten million pounds. However nice the prospect of winning a hundred million, it's not enough to balance the disastrous effect on the rest of your life of losing ten million. The ratio of downside risk to upside benefit is only part of what matters about risks. There are some risks which are so horrible to contemplate that no amount of benefit will justify them.

We only have one planet. It would seem unwise, and contrary to most peoples' perception of risk, deliberately to run any significant avoidable risk of making it unfit for human habitation. Because of the lead time in atmospheric change, this is what a George Bush 'wait and see' approach to global warming means.

We therefore have to release less CO_2. This means we must burn less fossil fuels. It is worth emphasizing that these are two sides of the same coin. Repeated discoveries of huge extra reserves enabled the energy industry to pour scorn on the first wave of environmental warnings, which concentrated on the finite limits of resources. But this ignores the other side of the coin. Even if the whole planet turned out to be made of hydrocarbons, greenhouse gas emissions would still put the same limits on our using them. However advanced our seismic techniques become they will not locate any new atmospheres into which to put CO_2.

SUSTAINABILITY VERSUS GROWTH?

Many economists and business people become nervous at this point, because it seems to imply that saving the environment means abandoning economic progress and the goal of improving living standards. The assumptions behind this can be summarized as:

Human welfare
depends on
Material standard of living
is proportional to
Consumption
is inseparable from
Production
requires
Resource (e.g. energy) throughput
causes
Environmental damage.

On this view, increasing welfare requires increased resource throughput, and therefore more environmental damage. If this is true, environmental and developmental concerns are inevitably opposed, and 'sustainable development' is a contradiction in terms.

Fortunately there is a solution. It is essential to be clear about how sustainability and development can be reconciled, so this section explains it in detail. The essence of the solution is to recognize that the relationship between welfare and resource throughput is far more complex than this model admits. All the linkages can be slipped, or decoupled – at least up to a point. Development will become sustainable if they are slipped far enough to allow welfare to increase at the same time that damaging resource throughput is brought back within the planet's carrying capacity limits. So how far is this possible?

Decouple human welfare from material standard of living

All the great world religions exhort their followers to live more simply and less materialistically: to free themselves from the shackles of material things and concentrate on inner values. These calls have always been honoured more in the breach than in the observance, and 'Vote for me and I will make you poorer' is not a promising political programme. It would be unwise to rely on these moral precepts to modify behaviour for the sake of the environment.

It would, however, be possible to reduce the enormous social pressures towards consumerism by tighter controls on advertising. A few years ago the European Commission floated the intriguing idea of a ban on advertising of products which damaged the environment.

Decouple standard of living from rate of consumption

Consider two families. One lives in a spacious traditional house, furnished with antiques, in a quiet enclave near the centre of a town. The other lives in a small modern house, furnished with modern furniture, on a suburban estate.

Despite being larger and more comfortable, the first house may cost less to heat than the second one because its walls are over twice the thickness and it has traditional heat-retaining features such as window shutters and boarding in the loft. It may also cost much less to maintain: its roofing, woodwork and so on may last over 100 years whereas modern equivalents may need major overhaul or complete replacement every 20 years or so.

Similarly the antique furniture in the first house was built to last virtually indefinitely, and the family may quite happily go for years without buying or discarding any furniture. In contrast the modern furniture in the second house, made from industrial materials such as laminated particle board and plastic mouldings, rapidly becomes scruffy in normal use and cannot be restored, easily breaks and cannot be repaired, and therefore needs to be thrown away and replaced every few years. (This is an energy as well as a materials issue because of the energy used in extracting the materials, manufacturing the furniture, distributing to households, collecting it back again and disposing of it).

The same pattern may apply to other energy issues. The first family may be able to walk to all commonly used amenities such as shops, schools and places of work and recreation,whereas the second family may need to make several car journeys every day just to get access to these. Consequently the first family may enjoy easier access to a wider range of options with no car than the second family would with two cars.

Overall the second family consume energy, goods and services much faster than the first, but probably enjoy a lower quality of life. The first family's quality of life is based on *possession*; the second family rely more on *consumption*. The point of the example is to show that a good standard of material living can be combined with small resource impacts provided durable capital items are preferred to disposables – provided the quality of life comes more from having than from consuming: as it were from capital rather than revenue, or from wealth rather than income. It also illustrates the converse: it is possible to have a poor quality of life even with high resource use.

Decouple consumption from production

Consumption and production are linked pretty much by definition. However it is possible to seek to avoid production which never results in consumption – in other words to try to avoid production of things that will never be used. This happens when producers misjudge markets, for example when a new product fails to find market acceptance or an established one loses favour.

The two effects may be telescoped into one: a new introduction being quickly overtaken and made obsolete by another one. The consumer electronics industry does this so often it seems deliberate. These effects are more likely during periods of rapid market change, which is therefore undesirable from a sustainability viewpoint.

Decouple production from resource input and waste production

This can be done in two ways. The first is to increase the efficiency with which production processes use resources, especially energy. The more efficiently energy is used, the less is needed for a given level of output.

The second method is to reduce both inputs and outputs by using the outputs again as inputs: in other words, closing resource loops. Recycling is the best known example of this. Reuse, for example of packaging materials, recovery of spare heat from one part of a process for use in another, or use of wastes as a fuel source, are other methods for closing the loop. As a rule of thumb the tighter the loop the better for sustainability: reuse is best, recycling next and energy recovery last – although circumstances can vary.

Decouple resource throughput from environmental damage

'End-of-pipe' pollution control technologies can reduce harmful emissions. However they often merely displace the problem. Flue gas desulphurization at power stations does reduce acid rain; but only at the cost of landscape damage from limestone quarrying, the extra energy used in it, a reduction in the conversion efficiency of the station and the production of a slurry which must be disposed of.

A more elegant approach is to switch from finite to renewable resources – ones which do not cause environmental damage because they keep on coming anyway. Hydro, wave, and wind power are part of the mechanism by which solar energy drives physical processes on earth. We can in principle tap into them without upsetting any global resource balances.

We do not always succeed. The potential cleanness of renewable energy does not give the civil engineering projects needed to harness it any magic immunity from environmental harm. Hydroelectric power schemes have caused enormous ecological damage the world over, and there is justified anxiety over the effect of tidal barrages on coastal ecosystems, and of wind farms on migrating birds.

'Biomass' energy from burning or digesting plant material is in principle the same. We are tapping into a sun-driven biochemical, rather than physical, cycle, but again we are not breaching a limit: all plant material finishes up burning or rotting anyway, so we are not seriously disturbing the natural cycle if we tap energy off in the process. Again, however, the virtues of the result do not guarantee the blamelessness of the means. Carrying capacity limits apply: we must not take biomass material such as timber or oilseeds so fast that we eat into the ability of the source to replenish itself.

How does biomass differ from fossil fuel? The chemistry is the same, the only difference is the time lapse between the plant fixing solar energy and our using it. But this matters; the planet has got used to these being locked up; releasing them upsets the balance – whereas burning current crops releases back. Burning crops is like taking last week's lemonade bottles back for the deposit. Burning fossil fuels is more like selling the family silver.

A SUSTAINABLE ENERGY PATH FOR THE UK

Thus the energy technologies for sustainable development are:

(1)   Using less by *obviation* (e.g. less energy-intense lifestyles)

(2)   Using less by increasing *efficiency* of use

(3)   Energy *reuse and recycling* (e.g. combined heat and power, heat pumps)

(4)   *Renewable* generation

There is immense potential for all these in the UK. In round figures, 25% of current consumption could be met from renewables by 2020, at prices comparable to current supplies. Nearly half of this would come from onshore and offshore wind, and about another third from biomass, principally wood waste, energy forestry and digestion of wet wastes, although oilseeds may also make a contribution. The remainder would be made up of hydro, wave and possibly tidal, geothermal and solar.

At least a further 25% of current consumption could be saved through efficiency measures, again without significant extra costs. The main technologies in buildings are better insulation, draught proofing, better control of heating plant and alignment to take advantage of solar heating. Generic industrial technologies such as higher efficiency motors and drives, process heat recovery and better process modelling, monitoring and control can help, as well as innovations in specific sectoral technologies. In transport, the third main area of energy use, technical vehicle efficiency improvements could achieve the 25%.

These add up to a 50% reduction in primary energy demand. This could be further increased by a move to combined heat and power (cogeneration) which can double the efficiency of conversion to electricity. And these figures take no account of any obviation, for example in change of lifestyle to reduce energy needs.

Estimates of this sort must always be treated with caution. Beneath the round numbers lurk many complexities and uncertainties. For example, the more we rely on renewables the more the intermittent and unreliable availability of many of them will become a problem, though not an insoluble one. Averaging out the fluctuations by attaching the greatest possible number of different renewables in different places to the largest possible grid will help. So will extending demand management to smaller users such as households, and efficiency measures in buildings such as high thermal mass and integrated building energy management systems will facilitate this.

Similarly, any blanket percentage figure for efficiency improvements covers a vast range of individual cases. It is not difficult to build houses that in the UK's climate keep themselves warm from passive solar gain and the body heat and minor appliances of the inhabitants, with negligible requirements for space heating. These houses need not even cost more than traditional ones since the extra cost of the energy efficiency measures can be offset by savings on heating installations. If all new housing were built to these standards, and major renovations required to get as close as practicable to them, the saving over a few decades could be 50% or more. Actual output will include some of these superinsulated houses and some good, indifferent and poor ones. The mix will depend on a great number of factors such as prices, rates of dissemination of knowledge and capacity in manufacturers and builders, and public perceptions and expectations.

Predictions of the scope for obviation are even more subject to uncertainty since they depend so greatly on public attitudes and beliefs. Only a small change in habits could produce a dramatic reduction in car use. Public opinion surveys suggest that most people think this would be a good thing. But the change in habits is not happening.

However even taking these uncertainties into account it seems the UK could cut its primary energy demand by around 50% within about 30 years without any dramatic collapse in living standards. However it will need to be made to happen. Renewables are currently only 2% of generation. The main reducer of primary energy demand is the collapse of energy-using industry.

The Government's preferred motor of change is choice in the market place. Let us therefore consider next how this works.

MARKET FORCES

Uptake of energy efficiency measures by energy consumers

Competitive pressures have undoubtedly made firms keen to cut energy costs, and thus created market opportunities for other firms to develop and sell energy saving technologies. The energy intensity – the amount of energy used per unit of output – of most industrial activities in market economies has been steadily dropping since the second world war.

However, huge technical potential for energy saving remains unexploited. Most companies fail to take many opportunities which are obviously cost effective. A problem with the former Energy Survey Scheme was that even companies which had selected themselves as being motivated enough to pay half the costs of a consultants' energy survey often did not implement many of the recommendations.

Short timescales

The reason is that very short timescales dominate company decision taking. Few companies make energy saving investments that take more than 4 years to pay back; 2.5 years is a more usual limit. Companies will also switch fuels for sake of short-term price savings even at the expense of increasing longer term insecurity.

This is a natural and inevitable consequence of the basic realities of commercial life; money and management attention are expensive and always in short supply. Only those energy efficiency investments that pay back very quickly have any hope of competing with other calls on finance; even these will not get funding if there happen to be more pressing needs; and they will not even be identified where there are higher priorities for management attention.

The British structure of financial markets and pattern of share owner-ship places intense pressures on companies to maximize short-term returns. Any public company which tries to take a longer view – which sacrifices dividend to research or strategic development, for example – sees its share price drop relative to asset value, and becomes vulnerable to hostile takeover and asset-stripping, which have seemed to be safer and better rewarded activities than innovation, creativity and strategic planning.

This is unlike the pattern in Germany and Japan where financial institutions regard themselves as long-term stakeholders and partners in the companies they invest in, and are prepared to back business strategies they believe in through years of low returns for the sake of longer term advantage.

Discounting and sustainability

But even if companies were able to make all energy saving investments which were cost-effective, this would still fall far short of what sustain-ability would suggest. The reason is the convention of discounting future costs and benefits in cost-benefit calculations and investment appraisal.

Remember the view within downtown Vancouver which I described earlier, where the building you are standing next to blots out everything behind just because it is closest. Discounting is like this: the closer something is (in time) the more weight it carries. Like a 30-storey building three blocks away hidden behind a ten-storey one next to you, a large cost in thirty years time is more than compensated by a small benefit next year.

However what matters for sustainability is the overall amount of resources used to achieve a given benefit. From Mother Earth's point of view the relative timing is irrelevant. This is like the view of the city from North Vancouver, where buildings appear in correct scale relationship. The thirty storey building will look about three times as tall as the ten-storey one even if it is half a mile further away.

Discounting means that projects which buy short-term gains at the expense of environmental costs which continue long into the future appear viable because the long 'tail' of costs are discounted. Discounting also means that it is not worthwhile to spend a little more initially on an investment such as a building to ensure a much longer trouble-free life, because even substantial maintenance, repair and replacement costs in 20 or 30 years time are discounted down to a very small 'net present value'. The result will often be much higher material, energy and waste costs (financial and environmental) over the lifetime of an amenity or building than if it had been built durably in the first place.

Externalities

Companies are only concerned with their own energy costs. They will load energy costs onto others wherever possible. An example is the UK's leading supermarket chain, Sainsburys. They are rightly proud of the energy efficiency within their stores. But for years they have been replacing stores inside towns with a smaller number of larger stores on the edges of cities where land is cheaper and distribution quicker and more reliable. The fact that this increases the fuel used by hundreds of shoppers' cars by much more than it reduces the fuel used by a few delivery lorries is not Sainsburys' concern.

Similarly, company fuel switching decisions are made on the basis of price rather than the implications for greenhouse emissions, security of supply or employment. A company may switch to coal imports, or convert its boilers to gas, to reduce its fuel bills. Neither the low wages and lack of safety precautions that make imported coal cheap, nor the resulting unemployment in British coalfields are relevant to the company.

Commercial rationality versus sustainability

All this is perfectly rational behaviour on the part of companies. Nobody should ask or expect them to behave any differently. The whole point of the competitive system is that companies that do not adopt the practices which current market conditions make most lucrative go out of business. But equally nobody should expect or assume that the decisions made by companies operating within the ruthless disciplines of what are mysteriously called free markets will bear any relationship to sustainability, or for that matter to any other socially or environmentally desirable outcome. In his book *The Green Economy* Michael Jacobs has coined the term 'the invisible elbow' to describe the clumsy and arbitrary way Adam Smith's invisible hand really operates.

GOVERNMENT POLICY

There is an old-fashioned view that governments are there to solve this sort of problem: to make us all behave in ways that none of us would choose individually, but which make us all better off if all comply – for example to make each of us refrain from robbing each other in the street for the sake of the general convenience of being able to move around in safety. Sustainability may be a new goal of policy, but the notion of government intervention to promote it is no different in principle from government intervention to secure any other generally desirable objective such as law and order or affordable health care. It is easy to identify the sorts of actions governments can take to promote sustainable energy.

Possible policies for sustainable energy

Governments can invest directly in renewable generation, or set up a system of tax breaks, soft loans and price support to make it commercially attractive to entrepreneurs, as in Denmark.

Governments can set high mandatory energy efficiency standards for buildings (as in Sweden) or vehicles (as in Japan, on and off), raise energy taxes and use them to finance subsidies for conservation (as in the Netherlands), or integrate power generation with a heat distribution system (much of Scandinavia). Governments can adopt land use planning policies to minimize the need for transport (the Netherlands again), invest heavily in public transport (most of continental Europe), promote non-mechanized modes (Freiburg, Copenhagen), and institutionalize the pursuit of energy efficiency in business (MITI's Energy Conservation Centre in Japan).

Taxation, level playing fields and the relative cost of resources and labour

More radically, government could review whether at our current state of economic development it still makes sense to concentrate taxation on labour and value-adding activities rather than on primary resources. In all the fashionable talk about 'level playing fields' it should be remembered that the relationship between the costs of labour, capital and raw materials is conditioned by the tax system and that this has grown up out of a series of historical accidents rather than by conscious design based on *a priori* principles.

A case can be made that the current system which continues to encourage employers to replace staff with automation at the price of increased resource use is perverse now we have endemic unemployment and a need to reduce resource use for sustainability. The EC's carbon tax proposals, and the fiscal framework already in place in Denmark, can be seen as first steps in this direction.

The relative effectiveness of these measures, the desirability of their social and economic side-effects, and the best balance or mix of them to apply, can all be endlessly argued over. But the possibility of them is beyond dispute. All of them are already being demonstrated in practice to a greater or lesser degree, and generally in economies stronger and more successful than the UK's.

The British government view

However the Conservative government which came to power in 1979 does not subscribe to the old-fashioned view that these questions are a legitimate concern of government. Rather than have social, environ-mental, distributional or other such political values, and adopt policies to attempt to achieve them, the government has deliberately left them to the market. Indeed it has worked hard and consistently to help the market overrun those parts of the energy economy which were previously the province of public policy. The only significant exception has been a doctrine of safeguarding security of supply, although this has amounted to little more than a wary eye on OPEC and a rationalization for subsidy and protection of the nuclear industry.

This policy of un-policy started as a reaction against the perceived failure of the previous regime of regulation and state control. Certainly this had its shortcomings. From a sustainability viewpoint, the statutory duty placed on the Central Electricity Generation Board to maximize the efficiency of *electricity* generation was a major one. This apparently sensible and innocuous provision was interpreted by generations of CEGB bureaucrats as meaning that the Board would be acting *ultra vires* if it accepted even marginal reductions in generation efficiency in order to design power stations to make the waste heat available for industrial or domestic use – even if, as would usually be the case, the result would be far greater overall efficiency of energy conversion. We thus have a legacy of huge thermal power stations only getting half of the possible useful energy out of the fuel because some parliamentary draughtsman was ignorant of the most basic thermodynamics, and nobody thought to put him right or challenge the results.

A story like this can make untrammelled free enterprise look almost rational. But the way we have gone to the opposite extreme reminds one of the Hungarian proverb that when you climb up one side of a horse it is easier to fall down the other side than to get securely into the saddle.

Privatization

Since 1979 the UK has privatized its public sector oil assets, the whole gas industry, the whole electricity distribution and supply industry and most of electricity generation. British Gas was sold off as one gigantic vertically-integrated enterprise. Following criticism that this merely turned an uncontrollably bureaucratic public monopoly into an uncontrollably predatory commercial monopoly, the electricity industry was split up into a number of regionally based distribution companies, two unequal fossil generation companies, a company to oversee the national grid and two vertically integrated generation and supply companies in Scotland. Only two bits of the electricity generation system – the nuclear power stations and the coal mines – remain in public ownership. More about them later.

The result has been to force onto the supply industry the same anti-sustainability pressures already noted on the consumption side. The energy companies are all forced by the logic of the market place to maximize short-term profits to satisfy their shareholders, to sharply discount the future consequences of their actions, and to ignore the social and environmental consequences.

Institutional arrangements

It has been nobody's job to worry about the implications of this. Parallel with the selling-off of the energy supply industries, the government machinery for energy policy has been progressively dismantled. Within the Department of Energy, the Energy Policy Division was first demoted from its former central position as coordinator of and arbiter between the divisions responsible for particular industries. It became a peripheral irritant and a dustbin for marginal issues which did not merit a proper home. (It is amusing to remember that circa 1984 both European affairs and environmental questions fell into this category: each was the subject of a small and unprestigious unit within Energy Policy Division.)

Then around 1985 the Energy Policy Division was simply abolished, on the grounds that energy policy had itself been superseded. Following each privatization the relevant industry sponsorship division was col-lapsed into a small caretaker unit. After the 1992 election the process reached its logical conclusion. The Department of Energy was abolished and the rump of privatization and liaison work left became merely one of a number of Deputy Secretary commands within the Department of Trade and Industry. Energy now has no cabinet representation of its own, and no parliamentary select committee: it is merely one of a large number of issues handled by the Secretary of State for Trade and Industry and the Trade and Industry Select Committee.

The Energy Efficiency Office was separated from the rest and attached instead to the Department of the Environment, thus further entrenching the lack of coordination between energy supply and demand policies which had already been a serious weakness.

Least cost planning

Consumer and environmental lobbies tried to get some support for energy conservation and renewables built into the privatizations. The most sustained campaign was for least-cost planning. In the US, each State utility regulatory commission can stop an energy company from passing the cost of a new power station on to its customers if it is not satisfied that building the station is the cheapest way to meet the demand.

One reason a proposed investment may be blocked is if there is a cheaper power station option. This is one of the reasons no new nuclear station has been built in the US since the 1970s. More interestingly from a sustainability viewpoint, it may be because it would cost the utility less to *reduce* demand by giving its customers insulation, low-energy appliances and/or energy management advice than it would cost to *satisfy* the extra demand by building new generation capacity. Many American electricity companies have indeed done this, and been allowed by the regulatory commissions to pass the costs on in fuel bills. The system is thus an elegant way to make behaviour which promotes sustainability profitable.

The British government resisted this proposal. The official reason was that the introduction of competition would provide such a powerful incentive to improve efficiency that it was unnecessary. Subsequent events have confirmed that this was as fantastical and baseless a claim as the analysis above of how market forces oppose sustainability above would suggest.

There were two real reasons. First, the ideologists of privatization were so opposed to any restraint of markets that they refused to accept the lesson of decades of US experience that strong regulation was necessary to make the behaviour of monopoly suppliers of essential services acceptable. The second, and more down to earth reason, was that the government did not want to do anything to reduce the potential profitability of the industry and therefore the proceeds of selling it.

(It may also have had something to do with the fact that Nigel Lawson, whose considered opinion as Energy Secretary had been 'conservation is not an energy source, I can't run my car on it', was still Chancellor, and one of the leading advocates of least-cost planning was the Association for the Conservation of Energy, which had cheekily contradicted Lawson by naming its journal about energy conservation 'The Fifth Fuel'.)

In any case the opportunity to build a powerful motor for sustainability into the structure of the privatized industry was deliberately not taken. The consequence is that the profitability of the fuel companies, and therefore the contentment of the large number of new small investors persuaded to buy shares in them, and the political credibility of the privatization programme, depend on the amount of power the companies sell. It was argued earlier that sustainability and prosperity do not have to be opposed goals. In the case of the energy supply industry the government has made them so.

Recently there has been a slight change of heart. An Energy Saving Trust has been set up, financed by the supply industries through what is effectively a government-endorsed levy on fuel bills. This is better than nothing, although the amounts of money involved are tiny compared to either supply industry profits or the scope for energy saving investments. Leading energy conservation figures are concerned that projects will be chosen more for fuel industry PR benefits than on the basis of need. And unlike least-cost planning the Trust can have no influence over whether the industry's own investment decisions take any account of environmental impacts. Indeed because it depends on the profitability which the fuel industries maintain by anti-sustainable decisions, it can be seen as an attempt to co-opt the conservation movement.

The Non-Fossil Fuel Obligation

Privatization has resulted in one scheme which is good for sustainability: the Non-Fossil Fuel Obligation or NFFO. Under this the government requires the distribution companies to obtain a certain amount of power from non-fossil sources. The total amount, and the way it is split between different sources, can be changed over time. The industry satisfies this requirement by inviting bids from would-be generators and signing contracts with the most competitive ones.

The scheme originated as a green figleaf designed to legitimate a requirement to buy a quota of *nuclear* power. It ends in 1998 because the European Commission objected to special treatment of the nuclear industry after this date. The Commission has indicated that it would not object to a renewables-only scheme running beyond 1998, but the government has not yet responded to this.

The cut-off date has had several unfortunate consequences. First, it has made prospective developers demand higher prices for their power to get a return on their investment within 8 years rather than the 30 or more the plant the plant will last. This has artificially made the renewables look more expensive.

Second, it has made developers try to cut corners in getting projects approved quickly. This has created unnecessary public opposition and distrust. Third, many projects which fail to get through planning hurdles quickly will be abandoned, artificially damaging the credibility of the renewables.

Fourth, it has forced developers to maximize power output regardless of other factors. Wind farm developers have had to go for the tops of exposed ridges in hilly landscapes. As Friends of the Earth have pointed, these are usually the most visible spots in areas of outstanding scenic beauty, so the effect has been to set proponents of sustainable energy at the throats of other environmentalists concerned with countryside aesthetics.

Whether any of these results were consciously intended by the privatization officials who framed the NFFO is a matter for speculation. But while it has undoubtedly helped stimulate renewables development in the UK, the way the NFFO has been set up has succeeded in importing some of the nonsenses of the market even into the renewables industry.

Scotland illustrates the NFFO's status as a nuclear figleaf. Scotland has the best renewables opportunities in the UK, and a long-standing need to diversify rural employment which exploiting them could satisfy. Yet the NFFO was never applied to Scotland because there was already a high proportion of nuclear generation, no need to encourage more, and a general glut of supply capacity which has led the electricity companies to lobby against any stimulation of renewable generation.

Bad publicity and threats of legal action by independent power producers have finally forced the government to issue draft proposals for a Scottish Renewables Order. But they can be paraphrased not too inaccurately or unkindly as seeking to support a few symbolic projects provided they are not in any serious danger of becoming commercially viable or of producing significant amounts of electricity.

Energy efficiency promotion

Increased public concern about the environmental effects of energy use have led to a resumption within the last year of the promotional and exhortatory activities which the government had virtually abandoned after the Energy Efficiency Year promotional campaign in 1986. Recent soft-sell advertisements apparently designed to encourage people to act to avert global warming are reminiscent of an embarrassed parent attempting sex education: flinching away from actually stating the horrible truth, and trying to disguise the vagueness and evasiveness with a lot of bluster about plain speaking and frankness.

The government has constructed a situation where the only action most people can take on global warming is to reduce their use of the products of a motor industry which is already laying off workers and screaming for government to stimulate demand, or of energy supply companies whose shares were sold to those same people on expectations of profits which depend on continuing high consumption. Since this is the case, the flinching from clearly stating the message is perhaps not surprising.

One of the clearest lessons of the 1986 campaign was that generalized endorsement of energy efficiency without specific practical advice has no measurable effect on people's behaviour. The current campaign raises the question whether this lesson has been entirely forgotten, or whether it has been learned all too well. The emasculation or abolition of the schemes of grants and assistance which had the most practical impact would suggest the latter.

NUCLEAR POWER

Government's treatment of the nuclear industry is an intriguing exception to many of the previous arguments, with a logic all of its own. First, it is the one energy industry which throughout the Conservative period has continued to receive unquestioning government support and subsidy on long-term policy grounds. This was originally justified on the grounds that it would be cheap, reliable and clean. As the evidence mounted that it was expensive, unreliable and polluting, instead of cutting support the government accepted industry arguments that if only we persevered it could be made sufficiently less expensive, less unreliable and less polluting to be worth having for the sake of security of supply.

This has been so unlike the government's usual practice of withdrawing support even from industries which *are* promising that even people whose experience in public administration makes them always prefer cock-up explanations begin to suspect a conspiracy. The enthusiasm of the Conservatives – supporting construction companies for big engineering projects, Mrs Thatcher's personal friendship with Lord Marshall, and 'institutional capture' by the nuclear industry of the division in the Department of Energy which was supposed to regulate it – may all have played a part.

The second way the nuclear industry stands out is that it is the only case yet where the privatization drive has instilled some common sense. The government was finally forced to stop believing the industry when advisers refused to proceed with the privatization of the electricity generation industry until the nuclear power stations were removed from the package because their poor performance record, high current costs and incalculable future liabilities made them unsaleable.

The nature of these future liabilities leads on to the third exceptional feature of the nuclear industry. Nuclear power is in an important respect technically unproven. Neither the long-term storage of high-level nuclear waste nor the environmentally safe decommissioning of a nuclear power station has yet been demonstrated. This major technical uncertainty sets nuclear apart not only from any of the fossil fuel technologies, but also from most of the renewables.

Moreover this uncertainty poses a particular sort of risk, which a comparison with one of the less technically proven renewables will illustrate. The worst possible outcome of the technical uncertainties of wave power is that it will prove impossible to make it work satisfactorily and economically, and the development programme will prove to have been a waste of money and to have prevented some highly talented people from doing possibly more productive work elsewhere. This would be regrettable and disappointing, but nothing more.

The worst possible result of the technical uncertainties of nuclear decommissioning and waste disposal, however, could be a release into the biosphere of extremely harmful substances at any point for hundreds of years, or a need for ruinously expensive measures to contain or prevent such releases, again at any point for centuries to come. This is not only a great deal nastier, it is also unavoidable. Once we have embarked on nuclear power there is no way we we can decide this risk is not worth taking and back out of it.

This indicates the fourth exceptional feature of nuclear power. Greenhouse gases are not the most important aspect of its environmental impact. (This is not to say that nuclear is free of greenhouse implications. The mining, treatment and transport of uranium and the construction and decommissioning of facilities all involve use of conventional energy. However these are smaller than the greenhouse implications of fossil fuel.)

The nuclear industry in the UK has pinned its hopes on the greenhouse case. A major charm offensive is already under way in preparation for the government's review of the industry in 1994. Nuclear power stations are sprouting visitor centres and wooing tourists with guided tours. The industry is providing well-groomed speakers for school conferences, and laying on lavish seminars at which academics of varying eminence, opinion-formers and would-be opinion-formers are deftly flattered by being respectfully consulted about policy development. The message, thoroughly researched and professionally presented, is always the same: that a rapid expansion of nuclear power is the only thing that can save us from having to choose between catastrophic global warming and the end of western civilization as we know it.

None of this has yet changed the visceral unease and distrust which most ordinary people feel for nuclear power. Three arguments already made in this paper suggest that it should not. First, the discussion about decoupling welfare from environmental damage shows that a reduction in energy demand need not inevitably cause the collapse of civilized life. There is the alternative of changing the direction of development to be less energy intense. For several years Japan combined a growing economy with an absolute reduction in energy demand. The measures which achieved this can be copied elsewhere. The figures quoted about the prospects for renewables show that the 'energy gap' identified by the nuclear industry can be filled more cheaply, by other energy sources without its problems.

Second, the argument about risk. The industry publishes statistics which suggest that the risk of nuclear power, expressed as fatalities and injuries per unit of power, is less than for other forms of energy. These figures are at best contentious: many have remarked how funny it is that the once-in-a-million-years accidents seem to choose so often to happen in the first twenty years of the million. But even if the figures are true, they are largely beside the point. Nuclear power is like the ten-million-pound wager described earlier: however large the *probable* winnings, they are not enough to make the *possible* losses acceptable.

Third, the discount argument. The long tail of liabilities for care and maintenance of nuclear waste dumps may vanish into the distance under the accountants' perspective of discounting. But looked at in sustainability terms it looms larger than the benefits. In terms of intergenerational equity it is a burden we have no right to impose on our great-grand-children's great-grandchildren.

The nuclear industry seeks to portray its opponents as naive, uninformed and irrational. The arguments above suggest a very different conclusion. Opposition to nuclear power may be rooted in a broader view of the development options available, and a deeper and subtler understanding of the nature of risk and the pitfalls of an accountant's view of time preference, than those which inform the industry's plans. The fact that many of those opposed to nuclear power may appreciate these arguments intuitively rather than articulately does not make them any less valid.

CONSEQUENCES OF THE POLICY OF UN-POLICY

The consequences of this policy of un-policy have been predictable since the electricity privatization started to take shape in 1987 if not before. Now they are becoming apparent the only surprise is that anyone is surprised.

The dash for gas

The UK has at least 300 years worth of commercially exploitable coal reserves, and comfortable overcapacity in coal-fired power stations. In contrast estimates of gas reserves vary between 20 and 60 years. Until recently there were no gas power stations in the UK because it was accepted that gas was a premium fuel which should be saved for the uses where it had special advantages. Now, however, the regional electricity distribution companies are building gas stations as fast as possible. This is partly because (on some costing bases) the gas is cheaper; it is also because the distribution companies want to make themselves independent of the fossil generators.

Because of its chemistry gas produces less carbon dioxide for a given amount of energy than coal. It also produces negligible amounts of sulphur dioxide. The generation industry says that these environmental benefits are one of the main motivations for the dash for gas. The claim to be concerned about acid rain would carry more weight had the industry not reneged on promises to fit flue gas desulphurization to coal stations. Likewise the claim to be concerned about global warming would be more plausible if it was making any serious attempt to get the most benefit from the gas by using it in small combined heat and power stations matched to heat loads rather than big cheap power stations on the coast where the gas comes in. The sustainability comparison between coal and gas is in any case more complex, as the next sections explain.

The coal crisis

The current coal crisis is a direct result of the dash for gas. Since overall energy demand and commitments to nuclear change slowly, more gas has to mean less coal. The electricity industry has refused to sign new contracts for coal. This deprives the industry of a large part of its market. British Coal was only following the logic of the market when it announced the closure of 31 of its remaining 51 deep collieries with a loss of 30,000 jobs. The government was quick to endorse this decision and pronounce the economic case for the closures unanswerable.

The government had some reason to expect to get away with this. After bringing down the (compared to what has followed) mild, pragmatic and compassionate Heath government in 1974, and trying to bring down the Thatcher government in 1983 the National Union of Mineworkers was still widely perceived as 'the unacceptable face' of trade unionism. The coal industry had shed more jobs a year over many years with barely a murmur of protest outside the communities directly affected. The government's economic policies were widely believed to have been causing more grievous damage to industry over many years, yet it had still been re-elected only a few months earlier.

The chorus of outrage from all sections of society including its own supporters took the government entirely by surprise. After trying to tough it out, threats of backbench revolt forced the government first into conceding a moratorium, and when this was not enough to quell the protest, into an even more humiliating agreement to a 'real' review of energy policy.

Sustainability consequences of the crisis

In the flood of warmth toward the miners it must not be forgotten that burning coal for power is bad for global warming and also for acid rain; that the size, design and location of our coal-fired power stations precludes much improvement of their environmental performance through co-generation (combined heat and power) or clean and efficient combustion technologies; that spoil heaps and old workings emit methane and can produce toxic run-off if not carefully and expensively maintained; and that for all its cultural richness coal mining is one of the most arduous, dangerous and unhealthy occupations left. In the long run, sustainability dictates a phasing out of coal as an energy source.

But an abrupt switch to gas accompanied by sterilization of our deep mined coal reserves may have consequences that are highly undesirable on sustainability as well as employment, balance of payments and security of supply grounds. The big question which we cannot expect market-driven companies to care about is, what do we do when our own cheap gas runs out? Most of the possible answers are pretty unappealing.

First, we may be able to replace it with gas from the former Soviet bloc. It is generally believed that the infrastructure is in such poor condition that this will result in huge losses to the atmosphere of methane, a far worse greenhouse gas than carbon dioxide. However nobody really knows how bad the situation is. No serious examination of these questions has been carried out. This is partly for the demand-side reason that there was nobody left in the night-watchman Department of Energy to take any interest in the results. There is also the supply-side reason that to save money the privatized gas and electricity industries have closed down the renowned research stations which would have had the strategic interest, technical resources, detailed industry knowledge and intellectual capacity to carry out such an analysis.

In any case, gas from the east is also likely to be expensive: the Russians, Kazakstanis and so on will by then have learned enough capitalist economics to know that the correct thing to do with a customer who has made himself dependent on your product is to push the price up. And even this is assuming that it will be possible to do reliable deals with, and construct and keep intact pipelines across, countries which are at best politically volatile and desperately short of energy themselves, and at worst disintegrating in bloody civil wars.

Second, we could turn to nuclear. This seems unlikely. There is no reason why public opposition is likely to decrease. Indeed it may increase as the arguments discussed above become more widely understood. In any case the lead time on nuclear power projects rivals even that of the global climate system. By the time any emerging 'energy gap' is perceived as serious enough to justify a nuclear response, it will be too late to start nuclear projects in time to make any contribution before other solutions will have had to be found.

Third, we could turn to orimulsion, a tar-based fuel from Venezuela. This fuel is as environmentally damaging as high-sulphur coal, with the addition of vanadium. The pollution inspectorate and government environmental agencies are trying to prevent its use at present. Unlike nuclear it can be brought quickly into play in response to any crisis in supply because existing coal and oil stations can easily be converted to burn it.

It will be ironic if market forces make us resort to a fuel as environmentally damaging as the brown coal whose burning in central Europe has become a symbol of communism's environmental irresponsibility. But irony has never stopped something bad happening. Since the government appears to be delaying introduction of its much-trumpeted Integrated Pollution Control system, our best hope for keeping orimulsion out will be pressure from the European Commission – provided its environmental policing activities survive the argument over subsidiarity and Maastricht.

Fourth, we could return to coal, but opencast rather than deep mined because it is cheaper. This would have all the sustainability disadvantages of deep-mined coal, and destroy cherished landscapes into the bargain. It is cheaper because it requires far fewer workers. The other side of the coin is that it produces far less social and employment benefits than deep mining.

If the various problems and barriers touched on combine to make all these options sufficiently costly or restricted in availability, it is possible that the dash for gas may in the medium term be good for sustainability by making encouragement of energy conservation and renewables more attractive and cost-effective. But this is a flimsy hope. On past experience it is more likely that any crisis of energy supply caused by the dash for gas and its consequences would be used by the government as a reason for disregarding the environmental consequences of one or more of the unattractive options identified.

SUSTAINABILITY'S BEST HOPE: THE REDISCOVERY OF POLICY

However the coal crisis has a deeper significance for sustainability. For the first time since 1979 the market-based policy of un-policy is under serious challenge from all shades of opinion, including many government supporters.

It is partly accidental that this has finally come to a head over pit closures. As already pointed out, the government had been getting away with worse for years. But not when so much else was going wrong. In the months before the closure announcement the government's economic policies had lost credibility over repeated false claims that recovery was under way as the recession visibly worsened. Then currency speculators had forced abject abandonment of the flagship policy of ERM membership during a day of high panic and confusion while politicians and officials gave the impression they were pulling all economic levers within reach at random and finding none of them were connected to anything. No coherent new economic policy had been put in its place.

At the same time repeated, disruptive and apparently arbitrary and pointless reorganizations of valued but crumbling public services such as education and health had helped create a general climate of uncertainty, unsettledness and apprehension about the future perhaps unparalleled outside wartime, but without any compensating sense of high purpose and shared endeavour.

Coming on top of all this, the suddenness of the pit closure announcement, and the government's apparent blithe disregard of its ramifications, has seemed to many people final proof that the state, having reduced itself to the role of night watchman, had now stopped patrolling or keeping watch, and fallen asleep in a corner.

Even if pit closures are only accidentally the ground of this debate they are appropriate because they demonstrate some simple but often disregarded facts very clearly. If a decision such as whether to have a deep mined coal industry is made purely on the basis of the current perception of commercial advantage by private companies, then *of course* no account will be taken of the effects on the 31,000 people who worked in the mines to be closed or their families and communities, let alone the 47,000 estimated to lose their jobs in industries supplying mine equipment and such like, or the 15,000 elsewhere in the economy likely to lose their jobs through the result of the drop in consumer spending, or the extra taxation or cuts in public services needed to finance the unemployment pay of these extra unemployed people, or their knock-on effects. *Of course* no account will be taken either of the consequences for the balance of payments, security of energy supply or sustainability.

If these things matter there have to be mechanisms to take them into account. They have either to be the subject of explicit political decision or, if market based approaches are preferred, the market framework has to be consciously managed and constrained so that social and environmental costs and benefits are made explicit and given due weight in decision taking. There has to be more to macroeconomics than the microeconomics of the individual firm writ large; and there has to be more to energy policy than either.

For the sake of sustainability, energy has to be made more expensive compared to other factors of production, and ways have to be found to make both energy supply and consumption decisions take account of longer term costs and benefits and environmental externalities. These will result in growth of renewables and conservation activities and a corresponding decline in nuclear and all forms of fossil energy. As they decline there may also be some switching between them, but this is a relatively minor question.

However this must be accomplished without unacceptable economic and social consequences. The current energy industries must be helped to move into the new energy businesses, or at least to diversify out of the declining ones. Energy costs must be raised in ways that do not amount to regressive taxation on lower income groups. Measures to discourage unsustainable lifestyles such as long car commuting journeys must not be introduced so suddenly as to make life intolerable for people who have made lifestyle decisions that appeared rational in the circumstances in which they were made.

Doing all this will not be easy. It will require an energy politics of conscious planning and endless debate, compromise, experiment, adjustment and reconsideration. This may seem tedious and unattractive to those who have become accustomed to a politics of simple certainties implying universal nostrums which will solve all problems provided they are applied ruthlessly and consistently enough. But recent events have started to show the poverty of this approach. We have to rediscover policy because – as a political force of the 1980s might have put it – there is no alternative.

Whatever the direct outcome of the coal crisis, if it re-establishes the old-fashioned view that government is there to have policies and to try to implement them, and that ministers cannot abdicate to any magic mechanism their responsibility for trying to reconcile the conflicting social, economic and environmental pressures that arise in a complex society, then we will at least be able to make a serious start on the difficult task of moving the energy economy towards sustainability.

4 The Role of Government Policies and Regulation in Energy Strategies

I   A View From Canada

Roland Priddle

Introduction

As they contemplate Canadian energy issues, British participants should bear in mind some of the political fundamentals of the country: a constitutional monarchy at the federal and provincial levels; a British parliamentary system; one of the world's least centralized federal states; federal responsibility for interprovincial and international trade and for works and undertakings (e.g. pipelines) which join the provinces to each other and join Canada to the USA; ten provinces and two territories; provincial ownership and management of non-renewable natural resources, and special constitutional provisions regarding provincial rights in the area of electricity; shared management of eastern offshore oil and gas resources with Newfoundland and Nova Scotia (separately); great East-West extent, resources eccentrically located, exports from the West (oil, gas and coal too), imports from overseas to the East (lots of oil, a little gas and important coal volumes); the need for extensive federal-provincial discussion of energy, environment and related matters if relevant policies are to be successfully developed and implemented.

Characterizing Canadian Energy

Canada has, relative to its small population, abundant resources of all fossil energy forms, hydraulic resources and uranium. On the other hand, these resources are not strikingly abundant, having regard to its great land mass (the second largest in the world), and the geological and topographical characteristics of that land mass.

A second feature is that, not surprisingly, Canada's energy resources are unevenly distributed. Their somewhat 'eccentric' distribution has had two consequences. Tensions have arisen, from time to time, between active producing areas (Alberta) and the major consuming areas (Ontario and Quebec) with negative political consequences within the confederation.

Additionally, geographical (the North) or technical (the oil sands) relative remoteness have prevented some resources from being brought commercially to market.

I would characterize Canada's energy resources as being 'extensive' rather than 'intensive'. By this, I mean that they occur over an unusually wide range of unit costs. At low prices, the supply will be small, while at high prices the supply of energy could be remarkably large. Thus, hardly any new oil or gas would be produced if an international oil price of, say, US$5/barrel ('B') played on the Canadian resource. Extremely large quantities would be available, including from the oil sands and frontiers, if Canada's oil and gas resources were subject to an international price environment of, say, $30/B.

What this means is that the development possibilities for Canadian oil and gas and other energies are very strongly affected by global trends, particularly of course the international oil price environment.

As well, because of her small population relative to the energy resource base, Canada has for many years been a net exporter of energy. This has made her vulnerable to 'access terms' for exported energy, whether oil, gas, electricity or uranium, in foreign markets, essentially the United States.

Three Decades of Canadian Energy Policy

At the federal level, energy policy has been subject to some remarkable 'swings' since the late 1950s.

Thus, the 1960s were an era of glutted international markets and slowly falling prices. In Canada, the potential for oil and gas development seemed to be very large. The federal policy response, endorsed by both of the principal political parties, was to encourage production and exports, particularly of crude oil.

The 1970s was, of course, an era of rising prices, with major price 'spikes' in 1973–74 and 1979–80. Without change of government, there was sharp change in policy, involving the inception of an era of energy nationalism, the creation of a state company and the 'cushioning' of Canadian consumers from the effects of international oil and energy price shocks.

A sharp and, as it turned out, final upward twist to this nationalistic spiral was given by the National Energy Program of 1980. For four years, the federal government's efforts were directed in costly, anti-economic and nationally divisive ways towards 'super energy nationalism '.

Since 1984, and the coming to power of a government dedicated to allowing market forces to have free play in energy, the regulation of markets has been largely dismantled and a strong market orientation given to national and provincial policies.

Privatization

'State capitalism' in Canadian energy has traditionally been restricted to the electricity supply industry in all provinces except Alberta and Prince Edward Island.

Privatization in this area has so far been limited to this summer's successful sale to private investors of the Nova Scotia Power Corporation. In this case, a modestly-sized coal-based generation, transmission and distribution utility serving a total population of about a million was sold by its provincial government owners for some $850 million.

The oil and gas industry had traditionally been almost entirely privately owned. However, a large national oil company, Petro-Canada, grew out of the energy nationalism of the mid-1970s. The company ranks among the top three integrated oil and gas companies in Canada. It has not been commercially successful. As a result of the partial privatization in 1991 and 1992, it is now approximately 30 percent privatized. It has, since the mid-1980s, been under government direction to behave as a private corporation.

Provincial government forays into the area of commercial activity in oil and gas production occurred in a number of jurisdictions (Alberta, Ontario and Saskatchewan come to mind). Again, it tended to result in the acquisition or creation of assets at high cost. Most have now been abandoned, some at substantial loss to the taxpayer.

The essential problem in Canadian energy privatization is twofold. First, to convince the public that the rationale for the state's acquisition/ creation of energy assets is no longer valid. Second, to maximize the value of the assets sold, which involves consideration of when to sell, how and to whom.

Colloquium participants recognized that, because of poor timing, Canadian privatazation had yielded less for governments and had been accompanied by less public enthusiasm than those undertaken earlier by the U.K. Timing, in turn, was a product of the eras in which privatization-minded administrations came to power in each country.

Regulatory Authorities

In discussing regulation, I shall limit myself to that which is peculiar to the energy industries. Other forms of regulation – for example, fiscal and environmental – are of course common to other mining and manufacturing sectors.

I might comment that UK participants tended to object that it is inappropriate to distinguish energy regulation from environmental regulation, which tends to be directed in large degree at energy emissions.

The regulation of markets, which economists now agree was almost entirely counter-productive to the economic best interests of the country, has, as I have noted above, been essentially abandoned.

The remaining market regulation which I mention is of long-term exports of oil (non existent), natural gas (continuing, and important) and electricity (currently rather small in quantitative terms).

This export regulation has a long history in Canada, extending to turn-of-the-century situations where the strength of American export demand for Canadian (natural gas) resources pre-empted supply for domestic markets and led to the start of a long tradition of reviewing whether the energy form to be exported is somehow 'surplus' to Canadian requirements.

This is a responsibility of the National Energy Board. We seek to exercise it in as light-handed a manner as possible. Essentially, we do this by satisfying ourselves that Canadians have equal opportunity with export buyers to purchase the resource in question and that its long-term commitment to export will not make it difficult for Canadians to meet their energy requirements.

Much remains by way of 'technical regulation'. Right across the chain of energy activity, for example from oil and gas production to retail distribution, safety is of course a concern of regulators. The same can be said of environmental protection, where our record is good but where constant improvement is striven for.

In regard to the 'upstream' petroleum industry, Canada, largely through its provincial agencies, has an excellent record of managing its petroleum resource in a manner designed to maximize return to the Crown, while still promoting development, and avoiding waste and pollution arising from exploration for and development of production of the resource.

Finally, there is comprehensive regulation in Canada of 'natural monopolies' in what I would describe as the American regulatory tradition. In cases where, for technical or other reasons, energy transportation and distribution facilities are not subject to the free play of competitive forces, government has substituted regulation for competition. This is done through regulatory boards at the provincial level and by the National Energy Board at the federal level.

A notable and fairly general exception to such regulation are most Crown-owned provincial electricity generation, transmission and distribution utilities (there are important exceptions).

The Colloquium discussion at times focussed on the question to what extent regulation, for example for environmental purposes, could be 'market driven'? UK participants tended to be sceptical. Canadian contributors felt that it is worthwhile to afford energy actors the opportunity of making choices, for instance by providing for tradeable pollution credits and by providing alternative means to meet environmental goals, such as fuel alternatives.

Future Relations Between Government and Industry

The change in government in September 1984, the subsequent accelerated dismantling of market interventions at the federal level, the elimination of discriminatory taxation on oil and gas, and the substantial removal of constraints on foreign investment in the energy industries has led to today's situation which I would characterize as one of essentially harmonious relations between government and industry and between various levels of Canadian governments in the matter of energy.

The removal of interventions and discriminations in the 1984–85 period was followed by a weak energy market which disadvantaged producers and advantaged consumers. However, by and large the Canadian industry did not seek comprehensive and continuing interventions by governments on the other side of the scale, designed for example to support prices or protect markets. Canadian governments did act cooperatively and energetically to improve market access for oil, gas and electricity. Interventions which took place since 1984–85 tended to be jointly between the two senior levels of government and to be related more to regional development than to energy supply (e.g. the Hibernia oilfield, offshore Newfoundland; the bi-provincial heavy oil upgrader on the Alberta/Saskatchewan border).

Canadian participants saw less need for interventions and policy actions directed to improve security of energy supply than did UK members. The latter's concerns related in large part to the potential insecurity of energy supply to Western Europe from the CIS, not a matter of direct concern in the Canadian context.

As for the future, I'm optimistic that, whichever party forms the next federal government or whether we see some kind of a coalition, the outlook is for reasonably harmonious government and energy industry relations. Factors contributing to this view are: the stipulations of the Canada-USA Free Trade Agreement; the moral commitments in relation to the International Energy Agency of the OECD; and the practical constraints of the international market for energy and capital. These are such as to limit the scope which future Canadian governments have for interfering in the energy industry in the sort of ways which characterized the late 1970s and early 1980s.

Government Policy With Regard to Greenhouse Gases

At the Second World Climate Conference held in Geneva in November 1990, Canada, along with a number of other countries, committed to take actions to stabilize greenhouse gases (GHG) concentrations at a level that would 'prevent dangerous anthropogenic interference with climate'. Specifically, the commitment was made to stabilize emissions of CO_2 and other greenhouse gases not controlled by the Montreal Protocol (chlorofluorocarbons – CFCs), by the year 2000 at 1990 levels. This commitment was reaffirmed by Canada, along with 153 other countries, at the United Nations Conference on the Environment and Development

(Earth Summit) in Brazil this year (1992) by adopting the United Nations Framework Convention on Climate Change with the following clearly stated Ultimate Objective: '...to achieve...stabilization of GHG concentrations in the atmosphere at a level that would prevent dangerous anthropogenic interference with the climate system...within a time frame sufficient to allow ecosystems to adapt naturally to climate change, to ensure that food production is not threatened and to enable economic development to proceed in a sustainable manner.'

In support of the Ultimate Objective, the Convention endorses the precautionary principle that 'Scientific uncertainty is not a reason for inaction'. All signatories are committed to report GHG emissions, to develop national GHG limiting programs and to develop, apply and transfer relevant technology, information and processes. Additionally, there is a commitment for developed countries to adopt policies and measures to limit emissions, to aim to return emissions of GHGs to the 1990 levels by the end of the decade and to provide new and additional resources to Lesser Developed Countries. These commitments are to be revisited by the end of 1992.

The Climate Change Convention Process agreed to by the 154 signatories undertakes a defined schedule over the period 1992–98 for review and reporting of progress in controlling GHG emissions.

In order to fulfil these commitments, Canada developed the National Action Strategy on Global Warming. This Strategy, developed in November 1990, was prepared under the auspices of both the Department of Environment and the Department of Energy, Mines and Resources. The Strategy has subsequently been confirmed in Canada's Green Plan. Its three main elements are:

(1)   Limiting net emissions of greenhouse gases;

(2)   Anticipating and preparing for global warming; and

(3)   Improving our understanding of global warming.

Federal-provincial agreements are to be negotiated to administer the emission reduction commitment; however, to date, no concrete mechanisms have been developed to curtail source emissions of GHGs and no agreements have been made between federal and provincial governments to cap emissions at the regional level. Initial actions are expected to focus on measures aimed at improving energy efficiency and promoting the shift to less carbon-intensive alternative energy sources. Other actions may need to be taken to ensure Canada meets its emission reduction target and this target may need to be adjusted downward as new scientific data become available and further international protocols are negotiated.

This contributor would certainly agree with those, in particular one Canadian politician, who forcefully argued that the GHG issue is a global one that requires global solutions; that pragmatic rather than esoteric solutions are needed; and that there is enormous scope for highly cost-effective international cooperation.

Possible Political Developments in or Affecting Canada

(1)   October 1992, Canadian Constitutional Referendum

(2)   November 1992, USA Presidential Election

(3)   Sometime 1993, Canadian Federal Election

(4)   Sometime 1993–94, Alberta Provincial Election (?)

The 'No' vote in #1 may produce an extended period of political and economic uncertainty: it has been a factor in the November 1992 fall in the value of the Canadian dollar which, however, has mildly stimulated the oil and gas producing industries whose output is related to pricing in international markets; #2 has brought about a change of Administration, which could result in greater government energy involvement and perhaps greater emphasis on particular fuels such as natural gas, thereby further encouraging imports from Canada; #3 could lead to a change in the colour of the Canadian federal administration; and #4 is potentially important because Alberta is, of course, Canada's energy province. However, energy policy is not an area of much disagreement between the principal parties there.

Speculation on the change which could result from the political milestones indicated above is practically boundless but, as I would see it, not particularly useful at this point in time. The only sensible comment which I feel able to make is that politicians' attitudes and initiatives will be influenced primarily by:

(a)   Their understanding of the public perception of energy issues;

(b)   Views, and possibly changing views, on the energy-environment nexus; and

(c)   Perceptions as to the 'extent of the possible' in terms of policy-change versus policy continuity, where attitudes will be strongly influenced by the strength or otherwise of the national and international economy.

Implications of Competition Policy

Competition policy has not been a major factor in Canadian energy.

Nearly a decade ago, an exhaustive study by the Federal Restrictive Trade Practices Tribunal responding to an adverse report by the Bureau of Competition Policy, found essentially no great grounds for concern about the state of competition in the downstream oil industry.

Figure 1   The Canadian (Federal) Energy Policy Environment
1947–1992   (Primarily Oil and Gas)

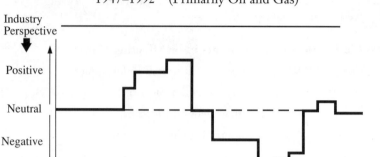

Gas transmission and distribution are essentially regulated monopolies, where the physical facilities and the return to private investors available from them are regulated by federal and provincial tribunals.

The market for natural gas has not been regulated since 1986, resulting in Canada now having probably the freest gas market in the world.

The state (i.e. provincial) electricity utilities are subject to oversight by their governments, and in some cases are subject to utility regulation much as are the gas utilities.

While the Bureau of Competition Policy at the federal level no doubt invigilates the operation of markets in all sectors of the energy economy, it has not so far had an active role in regard to the regulated sectors. Instead, control of monopoly has, as I earlier mentioned, been left in the hands of these specialized tribunals.

There is undoubtedly a rather high degree of concentration in the Canadian petroleum products industry. However, all of the indicators are that this is a strongly competitive business which yields rather low (some would say unacceptably low) returns to investors. The scope for exercise of oligopolistic powers tends as well to be limited by the important role which imported oil products supplies and independent dealers play at the margin of the market.

4 Role of Government Policies and Regulation in Energy Strategies

II The United Kingdom Case

John Harvey Chesshire

It is always interesting for economists to witness large-scale experiments, but I must admit to a feeling of relief that this particular experiment is not taking place in my own country.

Jean-Charles Rochet, University of Toulouse, 1991

Introduction

The announcement of another major round of colliery closures on 13 October 1992 was long anticipated by specialists tracking the dramatic changes occurring in the UK energy market, particularly in the strategically important power generating sector. However, the reactions it provoked in Parliament and in the country at large were not so readily anticipated by the Government as was soon admitted.

As a result of the tumultuous events over the past three weeks following the announcement, many elements of British energy policy are now under systematic and public review for the first time for more than a decade. The Government's review is being coordinated by the Department of Trade and Industry (the DTI which took over responsibility for the energy sector when the Department of Energy was abolished following the General Election). A quite separate enquiry is also under way by the House of Commons Select Committee on Trade and Industry. Specific elements are also being assessed by the electricity regulatory body, OFFER. On a wider front, other investigations have been under way for some time into related issues such as the UK's public sector nuclear decommissioning liabilities (by the National Audit Office) and into longer-term energy R&D and technology policy by the DTI's Energy Technology Support Unit (ETSU). Even before the present coal-related policy review, the Government had committed itself to an in-depth review of nuclear power policy in 1994 – elements of which may now be brought forward.

Thus, to accept an invitation to address a distinguished audience such as this at the present time of flux on the theme of UK energy policy was perhaps a little foolhardy! It must be admitted from the outset that perhaps no British participant to these proceedings possesses a crystal ball of sufficient quality to divine with any accuracy the outcome of these various policy reviews. On the narrow issue of the proposed pit closures, at present it appears difficult to identify sufficient degrees of freedom in policy terms to suggest that the outcome of this element will radically influence the prospects of deep-coal mining over the next decade. A stay of execution may well be possible for some of the threatened 31 pits. This depends crucially upon an unpredictable amalgam of political will, policy fudges and, perhaps, some regulatory flexibility. But the combination of market realities, electricity (and coal) privatization, diminishing geological reserves of economically recoverable coal and the ever-present environmental pressures deriving both from acid rain and global warming suggest that UK coal output will decline steeply over a longer time frame.

For much of the past decade, I have argued the case for more explicit attention to be given to an energy policy framework for the UK. This was because, in the absence of such an approach, there was a danger that individual decisions – whether on the pace and form of privatization, longer-term R&D policy or on reactor choice – would be taken in an ad hoc way. Recent events have confirmed that judgement.

Although international energy markets are at present more relaxed than they were in the 1970s, in my view it would be unwise to be complacent about the strategic role of the energy sector in modern industrialised economies. The supply security issues which dominated the uncertain 1970s will thus remain important, but environmental constraints are likely to play a much greater role in shaping the energy policy agenda. Privatization of the gas and much of the electricity supply industries has to some extent reduced the options available to the UK Government, but the European Commission will become more assertive in the context of the Single Market.

Finally, let me apologize for the fact that this background paper has been prepared in some haste as a result of the welcome invitation to replace Robert Priddle at such short notice. Given the circumstances we face in the UK and the extraordinarily fortuitous choice of subject for the 1992 Canada/UK Colloquium, I have chosen deliberately to place emphasis on the government policy element of the topic I was asked to address in the main part of my text. Recognizing the nature of the current policy debate, and its origins in the role to be played by British coal in the large power station market, I have also briefly addressed some unresolved issues arising from electricity privatization. This is aimed to provide further contextual information for our Canadian colleagues.

Privatization Developments

Perhaps of most interest to Canadian participants, and certainly of greatest relevance to current UK policy debates, is the bold move to privatize much of the UK's electricity sector (the ESI). Without reservation the privatization of the ESI proved to be the largest, most complex and strategically most sensitive of all the privatizations embarked upon by the four successive Conservative Governments since first taking office in 1979.

Over the past decade, these administrations have transferred to the private sector wholly, or partially, the publicly-owned assets in British Aerospace, British Steel Corporation, Cable and Wireless, Amersham International (radio-chemical services and products), National Freight Corporation, British National Oil Corporation, Associated British Ports, British Rail Hotels, the on-and off-shore oil assets of British Gas (to form Enterprise Oil), Sealink (Cross-Channel) Ferries, Jaguar Cars, the Rover Group (formerly British Leyland), British Telecom, British Gas, British Airways and the publicly-owned water boards – not to mention Rolls Royce, British Shipbuilders, Royal Ordnance and substantial sales of publicly-owned council housing and most of the ESI. In addition, it is the Government's intention to proceed with sale of British Coal and British Rail in the near future.

Not surprisingly, therefore, *The Economist* has argued that '…Britain is the biggest and most advanced laboratory for the testing of privatization…' in the world at the present time.

When the 1979 Conservative Government took office, the proportion of UK final energy consumption met by private sector energy suppliers – essentially the multinational oil industry was about 41 per cent. With the sale of Britoil, Enterprise Oil, Wytch Farm and especially British Gas, this rose to about 73 per cent. Following the privatization of the non-nuclear elements of the ESI in Great Britain it rose to about 83 per cent. Virtually all of the remaining 17 per cent of public sector energy assets is accounted for by the nuclear stations in England, Wales and Scotland, the non-generating elements of the ESI in Northern Ireland, together with British Coal, the UK Atomic Energy Authority and British Nuclear Fuels Ltd.

As well as partially satisfying the Government's political desire to 'set the economy free', the revenue obtained (some £45 billion) from this sustained – but politically controversial programme of sales of publicly-owned assets has been of great importance for the Government's wider macro-economic and fiscal policy objectives, especially in financing lower rates of personal direct taxation and containment of the Public Sector Borrowing Requirement (PSBR).

Without doubt, the biggest jewel in the whole series of privatizations was the ESI in England, Wales and Scotland. By any definition, the British electricity industry is vast in scale – the former CEGB was second only (in the non-Communist world) to Electricité de France in terms of assets, generating capacity and sales. The combined total of net assets of the ESI in Great Britain (i.e. excluding Northern Ireland) prior to the flotations was £42 billion on a current cost basis, with 63 GW of generating capacity and annual operating income in excess of £12 billion in FY 1987/88.

ESI Privatization: The Specific Political Justification

Other than party political ideology, four principal justifications were advanced by the Conservative Government at the time of the privatization White Papers (in February and March 1988) to support the flotation of the ESI. They were:

(1) economic:
- to stimulate competition;
- to raise efficiency;
- by implication to contain costs (or even to reduce prices);
- to increase accountability by market exposure.

(2) political:
- to 'roll back' the influence of the State and to unleash entrepreneurial spirits;
- to foster wider share ownership and to 'give the people a stake' in a key industry.

(3) administrative:
- to reduce the size of the Civil Service;
- to stop civil servants 'second guessing' the industry.

(4) financial:
- to assist the Treasury (the Public Sector Borrowing Requirement) by reduced calls on public expenditure for electricity investment; and
- to raise a substantial sum via the proceeds of the various sales.

In reality, of course, it would have been surprising indeed had these justifications not been overlain by a further set of essentially political considerations. These included:

- pressure on the Parliamentary timetable which might dictate that radical structural alternatives (e.g. greater fragmentation of generation) could not be considered feasible;

- the powerful vested interests of the existing organizations comprising the ESI, particularly the CEGB and the ESI's trades unions;

- the sheer scale of the ESI and the need to ensure that the City could accommodate such a major asset sale (especially after the earlier difficulties in placing the Government's holding in BP);

- concern about the safeguarding of existing nuclear power installations, and the Government's original desire to see an important future role for nuclear power generation; and

- concern within the Conservative Party, and elsewhere, that the earlier large utility privatizations (British Telecom and British Gas) had met with a variety of criticisms, particularly as regards the merits of privatizing former public sector monopolies in a structurally unreformed manner.

Core Fluctuations of the Electricity Business

There are five core functions of any ESI and, inevitably, these played an important role in the process of privatization and will continue to influence the nature of the subsequent regulatory regime. These are:

(1) Generation
(2) Transmission (at high voltages)
(3) Distribution (at low voltages)
(4) Supply; and
(5) Ancillary services, such as metering and billing;
      customer relations and service standards;
      showrooms and appliance sales;
      and electrical contracting services.

In addition, however, given the special character of the ESI in modern industrial economies, the broader strategic functions of the industry are also of prime concern to any Government. These core functions tended to be ignored in the immediate financial and media interest surrounding the flotations. Briefly, these include:

– acting as the 'swing' energy market at times of supply crisis – e.g. fuel switching via the merit order to ensure supply security; carrying surplus capacity in the event of plant outages, and uncertainties relating to load growth and the vagaries of the weather;

– acting as the principal market for other core industries, including indigenous coal mining, nuclear construction and heavy electrical engineering. EC policy on procurement will in time weaken the strong producer/user relationships in the power sector; and EC policies on State Aids will have a similar effect in relation to domestic coal supply and the transitional safeguard provisions currently cushioning the nuclear industry;

– given the share of total emissions (especially of SO_2 and CO_2) attributable to the ESI, serving as the leading edge in the control of environmental emissions – a field in which the UK has for too long been seen as a laggard elsewhere in the EC; and

– through its considerable R&D programme, giving support to the nuclear, heavy engineering and the electrical appliance and equipment industries.

Key Issues for the Government and the ESI

In my judgement, the failure to resolve satisfactorily the way in which privatization would impinge on these strategic roles of the ESI has contributed to the present difficulties faced by the Government. Others would argue, perhaps, that it was not privatization as such but rather the specific – essentially duopolistic form adopted both in England and Wales and in Scotland.

Inevitably, the new structure and regulatory system represent a compromise between various policy objectives, structural alternatives and feasible technical options. They recognize that local distribution and transmission activities are effectively natural local and national monopolies. However, the Government believes that, as generation of electricity is not inherently monopolistic, there is merit in seeking to encourage competition – not only between the large incumbent generating companies but also from a range of new entrant generating companies (including the 12 Regional Electricity Companies, RECs).

Nevertheless, the structures introduced for both Scotland and England and Wales are essentially duopolistic in character. This will necessitate a framework of regulation which will embrace the five principal areas of generating (both environmental and economic regulation), transmission, distribution, supply and final customer service quality. However, the Government judged that generation would become competitive and thus that the scope of regulation in this field would be skeletal.

Whilst privatization was of the utmost importance for the Government and the ESI, in essence the form and structure of ownership could be described as being of only marginal significance to the wider range of core economic, environmental and technological issues facing the industry. They were not removed by the transfer of assets from the public to the private sectors.

The present unease amongst specialists about security of supply issues in the ESI is unlikely to go away. In particular, what plant can a competitive ESI order (say from 2000–2005) when incremental gas for power generation may either not be available or too expensive? Nuclear power looks unlikely in a competitive, vertically-disintegrated, non-franchised and risk averse ESI and coal may be seen as dirty given lack of earlier research on clean coal technologies. Thus the current 'golden scenario' of new entry based on gas-fired, low capital cost, environmentally friendly CCGTs could be relatively short lived. It appears the stakes in a capital-intensive, fuel-intensive, pollution-intensive – and especially a competitive – ESI are high.

In my opinion the wider roles of the ESI have not yet been satisfactorily addressed and, until they are, they will continue to pose stresses as the new system beds down. Examples include the special support mechanisms the UK Government has been forced to introduce to protect the nuclear industry from exposure to competition in the bulk electricity generating 'pool' – support which contrasts markedly with the lack of any similar support at present for the UK coal industry which is facing immense difficulties in the absence, as yet, of *any* coal supply contracts with the ESI after March 1993. Important though competition may be in controlling costs, competition will not necessarily safeguard these wider industrial and supply security concerns which remain of crucial importance to the UK economy and to the longer-run interests of electricity consumers.

Amongst the more sceptical observers, within and without the ESI, the Civil Service, the media and politicians of all persuasions, there remains some concern as to whether the outcome of privatization will be any better than the pre-existing structure in terms of 'bottom up' issues such as electricity prices, security of supply and customer service quality. Clearly this is not the place for exhaustive analysis of such issues and time is needed for the new creation to show its form.

Suffice to say that the Conservative dominated House of Commons Select Committee on Energy, after a long and wide-ranging inquiry into the Government's proposals, could only conclude that:

> 'Reviews of international experience, particularly of the USA and other European countries, do not reveal any strong, or indeed positive, correlation between, on the one hand, utility structure, form of ownership, and the degree of competition, and the level of electricity prices and overall utility performance on the other'.

If there are real – rather than ideological, political and fiscal – advantages to be derived by the majority of consumers from electricity privatization, they have yet to be made manifest. Perhaps this judgement will be viewed as harsh because of its premature nature. Time will tell!

Some Wider Energy Policy Priorities

With this foregoing discussion as topical context, let me now turn to a review of some of the core issues which I believe the Government (and by extension the European Commission) will need to bear in mind as policy for the energy sector is reviewed over the next few months.

The Case For and Elements of An Energy Policy Framework

The first priority I wish to review is for wider public debate about an energy policy framework for the UK and, by extension, the wider European Community. For too long, in my view, the core concerns of energy policy have been absent from the wider political agenda in the

UK. The last White Paper on Energy Policy was published in 1967[1], the last consultative Energy Policy Green Paper in 1978[2].

Since then, Ministerial statements relating to the energy sector have appeared *ad hoc* in character, focussing solely on the narrow issue in play (such as approval of the Sizewell B PWR reactor, or the capital reconstruction and subsequent rationalization of British Coal) with no reference to the wider context. In addition, whilst other Government departments (such as Transport) have seen value in publishing illustrative projections, the former Department of Energy – virtually alone in the OECD bloc – eschewed producing anything akin to a substantial forward look (at least for public consumption) since its evidence to the Sizewell Inquiry nearly a decade ago.

Given the long lead times involved in energy supply investment, planning lies at the heart of corporate life in the energy sector. The Government should thus not feel embarrassed to admit to doing likewise. The reluctance of the former Department of Energy to publish an integrated and quantitatively based policy framework may reflect the recent lack of policy concern about security of supply, other than during the war to liberate Kuwait, as much as the philosophical predilections of the Government which seeks to maximize the scope for market-based structures and solutions.

Relaxed international energy markets, especially since the fall in oil prices since 1986, have led to the view in some influential quarters (in the UK but more widely, too) that energy is but another traded commodity – like baked beans or toothbrushes – and hence devoid of significant policy content.

It is perhaps because international energy supply security has been off the agenda that structural reform and privatization have been able to assume such central political significance over the past decade. It is against this background of comparative calm in international energy markets that we have witnessed privatization of key energy industries since 1986.

The transformation of the UK energy sector from public to private ownership outlined above is clearly of some significance as regards the issue of instrumentality of policy in the UK (i.e. why and how Government can intervene, even if it chooses so to do). Together with the greater role now assigned to Community institutions, privatization will inevitably influence the character of energy policy formulation and appropriate policy instruments in future.

These dual transformations – at both national and Community levels – have led to a perception amongst some that government has no responsibility for the conduct of energy markets. But even the briefest analysis of international experience reveals that virtually all other OECD Governments are conscious of the need to encourage and/or coax energy markets periodically by setting out their own strategic perceptions –

particularly over longer time periods than energy markets, motivated by the search for short-term returns and deploying high discount rates, might normally consider.

Despite the considerable changes in energy circumstances and differences in emphasis adopted by successive governments, a core of policy imperatives have been important in the UK energy sector over the past 20 years. In my view they are likely to retain continuing significance. They include the following twelve elements:

- the provision of adequate, low cost, but secure energy supplies;

- seeking some stability in energy prices (overall and between fuels – sometimes by specific fiscal measures, e.g. the Gas Levy and three successive 10 per cent increases in real gas prices introduced in the 1980s);

- a framework of pricing and other financial controls (e.g. Financial Targets and External Financial Limits on the nationalised industries); given recent privatizations, these specific instruments will be of much less relevance in future but they have been replaced by a range of economic regulatory regimes for both gas and electricity of the RPI-X+Y kind[3] and the Fossil Fuel Levy – a subsidy to support the nuclear industry, especially to meet 'back-end' liabilities for reactor decommissioning;

- influencing investment especially within the nationalised energy industries, but also more widely through licensing or planning consents for private sector power stations, off-shore oil and gas fields, and refinery projects;

- taxation policy, especially at present to capture profits arising from UK Continental Shelf oil and gas development; but in future energy and/or carbon taxes are likely to be used as market-based instruments to influence the direction of inter-fuel substitution and to curb energy demand growth and emissions;

- issues relating to employment, safety and welfare in the mines, power stations and off-shore;

- a burgeoning framework of environmental regulation and inspection (e.g. for oil spills, acid rain, lead in petrol, nuclear waste disposal and global warming);

- research and development, and technology choice, especially for nuclear power and renewable energy sources – as much as instruments for industrial policy as energy policy;

- related industrial policy questions regarding equipment supply (e.g.

the Government's Off-shore Supplies Office but also the recent Community Directive on equipment procurement policy);

– net energy trade and its impacts on the balance of payments and the £ sterling exchange rate (especially against the US dollar, in which currency internationally-traded oil and coal are denominated);

– increased but, in my view, still insufficient Government encouragement to stimulate more efficient energy use; and, especially with an ageing population, greater attention to the social policy dimensions of energy use for those facing 'fuel poverty' and high energy bills in cold weather.

Clearly, some of these policy 'ingredients' are specific to the energy sector. Others form part of wider macro-economic, environmental, industrial, social or transport policy but have a direct bearing on the conduct and evolution of energy markets. The key point is that, just because much of the energy sector is now in private ownership, it will not necessarily reduce the wider national or European Community interest in a complex web of energy policy imperatives. If for no other reason, global environmental constraints and residual national and EC interest in strategic supply security will not permit inaction by governments and international agencies.

The Need for Policy Integration

In my view, the second requirement is for the various energy-related policy strands to be integrated much more successfully and in a forward-looking manner. Two examples – one national, the other European – perhaps best exemplify this point.

At the UK level, in the recent Environment White Paper[4], the Government recognised the need to:

'ensure that its policies fit together in every sector; that we are not undoing in one area what we are trying to do in another; and that policies are based on a harmonious set of principles rather than a clutter of expedients'.

Despite this fine declaration of intent, numerous policy conflicts remain to be resolved as recent events have revealed. A clear example is the view that expenditure on roads is an investment in infrastructure, but that similar expenditure on railways is a subsidy. Thus in the wake of the Government's Environment White Paper what is now needed is more effective policy development and its closer integration in the way the Government itself has suggested.

At the Community level, relaxed energy market conditions have enabled the Commission to place much greater weight upon one specific dimension of policy – that relating to competition and free trade. However, emphasis on the competition dimension of policy cannot mask the fact that complex 'policy triangulation' is essential, both by the Commission and national governments, between three inter-twined (but not obviously harmonious) policy thrusts. Probably the most salient potential policy conflicts may be characterised briefly in the following way:

(1) the DG IV (Competition Directorate) 'free market' thrust – regarding issues such as transit through Member States, Third Party Access, common carriage, equipment procurement, and pressure to reduce State aids in the energy sector;

(2) the DG XI (Environment Directorate) thrust – relating to policy interventions (through physical or fiscal means) in areas such as acid rain, the Large Combustion Plants Directive, installation of Flue Gas De-Sulphurization, lead in petrol, catalytic convertors, fuel quality standards, CO_2 and global warming; and

(3) the DG XVII (Energy Directorate) thrust – embracing the traditional core energy policy agenda items such as the degree of import dependence, and the achievement of energy supply security and fuel diversity within the Community.

Balancing Policy Emphasis on Demand and Supply

The third need is to seek to address a fundamental inconsistency which has lain at the heart of British energy policy for much of the past 50 years. This is the imbalance in the policy attention devoted to energy *demand* as opposed to energy *supply*. Experience has demonstrated that it is usually easier for powerful, long-established, vested interests on the supply side to organize themselves than for the relatively new and fragmented players in the energy efficiency sector.

Briefly put, development of the UK's coal, oil, natural gas and nuclear power resources have in the past often been viewed in their fullest *macro-economic* contexts, as can be seen from close scrutiny of the Plan for Coal (1974), the new nuclear power programme (1979) and the protracted debate about gas imports from the Norwegian Sleipner field (1984–85). Issues considered pertinent to these grand supply-side decisions included import dependence, supply security, the balance of payments, employment, industrial and technology policy, and public expenditure and fiscal policy.

Conversely, the strategic and macro-economic justifications for a more vigorous energy efficiency policy have been almost entirely unrehearsed. If energy efficiency has been seen within any wider policy context at all, that context has been essentially *micro-economic* in character – focussed almost exclusively on the family or corporate 'bottom line' as measured by improvements in household comfort, disposable income or company profitability.

A combination of pressing environmental constraints, a prospective return to significant energy import dependence, and increased competition in international (and especially Community) trade suggest that the UK urgently needs to address the significant economy-wide benefits of a high-profile, integrated and consistently applied energy efficiency programme. In this context a key issue is the unlocking of receipts from council house sales to boost job creation in the construction industry perhaps partly via an insulation retrofit programme for an ageing housing stock.

Assessing Longer-Term UK Energy Demand Requirements

Despite the absence of official demand projections, there appears to be general agreement that UK energy demand growth will be relatively modest for the foreseeable future. Partly this reflects the current sobriety about economic growth prospects but other factors are likely to be important, too. These include continuing structural change away from energy intensive, 'smoke stack' sectors such as iron and steel; market saturation effects (e.g. consumer durables); further efficiency gains via underlying processes of technical change and capital stock rotation in plant, equipment, vehicles, buildings and appliances; and the wider diffusion of more sophisticated electronic metering and controls.

Compared with demand forecasts made as recently as a decade ago, which suggested continued growth in UK primary energy demand at rates as high as 2–4 per cent a year, recent studies suggest a much flatter trajectory for overall energy demand. Indeed, estimates by reputable analysts suggest that continued economic growth could occur in the UK without significant further increments in energy demand (at least outside the key transport sector – discussed more fully below). This view is shared by numerous international agencies, too, at least for the industrialised OECD bloc as a whole.

The sector in which demand uncertainties appear greatest is transport. A decade ago, the ranking order of final energy demand sectors was (i) industry, (ii) households, (iii) transport and (iv) public and private services and agriculture. By comparison transport is now the largest single final demand sector, responsible for nearly one-third of UK delivered energy demand and still experiencing sustained growth. Apart from the railways, energy demand within the transport sector is also oil specific and thus of strategic importance.

To date, policy intervention in the transport sector (in the UK and elsewhere) has been much muted by the recognition that motorists have votes. Tentative moves to reduce fiscal incentives for gas-guzzling company cars, combined with growing awareness of the need to encourage modal shifts to public transport (especially in urban areas), may serve to rein back energy demand for transport. However, further fiscal intervention – especially to encourage choice of more fuel efficient vehicles – will be an essential component of both energy efficiency and environmental policies in the 1990s.

History has taught that it is more than a little hazardous to be confident about energy demand trends. Nevertheless, the battles during the 1970s between exponents of the 'high' and 'low' energy demand growth schools appear to have been replaced by growing consensus about UK energy demand trajectories over the next few decades. However, if strategic threats such as supply security or global warming are to be tackled, even if only in a precautionary way, the demand side is likely to emerge as the 'leading edge' of energy policy debate. Thus regular assessments of UK demand trends should be published by the Government to enable it to track national performance in meeting targets both for energy efficiency and environmental emissions.

An Energy Resource Assessment for the UK

Given the comparative energy resource wealth of the UK (in terms of fossil fuels, nuclear operating experience and renewable energy potential), it is perhaps surprising that there is still no central, official source of reference about the nation's energy reserves and the likely costs of exploiting them. Instead, one is forced to keep abreast of many sources – e.g. the Brown Book[5] (for oil and gas), and a stream of reports from bodies such as ETSU about the UK's renewable energy potential.

As a result, rather sterile debate continues regarding the economic size of indigenous coal reserves or the ability of UK Continental Shelf gas reserves to support a large programme of combined cycle gas turbine (CCGT) construction without resort to additional gas imports. Whilst specific studies will remain important, in my judgement there is a pressing need for their supplementation, say every five years, by more comprehensive assessments of UK energy resources (and the assumptions upon which they are based) as a key point of departure for both energy debate and planning by government and the fuel industries.

Corporate and National Interests – The Case of Coal

There is now wider recognition, especially in the mining industry, that data on physical reserves are of little consequence if the national resource costs of exploiting them are higher than those for internationally-traded alternatives. However, in my view, the pendulum may be in danger of swinging too far the other way. To take the obvious topical case, perceptions of short-term and narrow corporate commercial advantage –

coupled with pre-contract negotiation posturing by the main protagonists – are unlikely to provide a sensible basis for determining coal supplies for the power generation market during the 1990s.

As Lord Wakeham, the former Secretary of State for Energy recognised, it will be necessary to put in place longer-term coal contracts if British Coal is to be privatized. The flotation prospectus would be hollow without them. The present purpose is not to enter that debate but to highlight the absurdity of the present position between dominant (essentially duopolistic) coal-using utilities and a dominant (effectively monopoly) indigenous coal supplier. Formal training in economics is not required to appreciate that, with such a structure, normal rules of competitive market behaviour will not apply. We would be better served if this were openly recognised by all parties to the current controversy.

Of course, wider considerations will apply to such complex negotiations (largely whether or not the Government now chooses to assist in shaping them) including:

– the degree of geographical protection enjoyed by British Coal in terms of delivery costs to inland power stations; and the extent to which this could be eroded by the planned new coal import terminals;

– the scope for further cost-reducing technological and organizational change in British deep mines;

– the volatility in the dollar-denominated price of internationally-traded coal, and especially in the sterling/dollar exchange rate, as witnessed over the past decade (roughly in the span of $2.40/£ to $1.05/£ – an enormous range);

– the comparatively small quantities of steam coal traded in the international, sea-borne, market (some 160 m tonnes in 1991, half of it already shipped to European Community markets);

– the possible emergence of a 'low sulphur premium' in response to European and US Clean Air legislation;

– the fact that the 'coal chain', from export mine to consuming site, is long and complex with all players keen to extract profits (be they mining companies, railroads, ports, shippers, insurers, local and national governments etc); and, finally,

– of some concern to the European Commission in the context of the level playing field sought within the Single Market, the possibility that comparatively low-cost indigenous Community coal capacity in Britain could be closed whilst very large subsidies continue to be applied to much higher cost German coal supplies.

As is often the case, but particularly so at the present time of policy flux, it is difficult to anticipate the precise set of circumstances and inducements which will be used to reconcile such unseemly and open conflict as currently persists in the UK between the two vital industries, coal and electricity. It is much to be regretted that no obvious mechanism exists at present to reconcile private corporate and wider national interests in this and other crucial policy fields. But it is not unreasonable to hope that common sense will prevail, and soon, and perhaps as a result of the energy policy reviews now under way. With most of the electricity industry privatized, and coal privatization planned soon, it appears that the Government will not find it easy to 'square the circle' as it prepares the promised White Paper on Energy Policy.

Summary and Conclusions

To conclude, the latter part of this paper – reviewing some UK energy policy priorities – has argued for:

(1)   an energy policy framework to reflect and shape corporate, government and European Community approaches to the energy sector;

(2)   more effective policy integration, especially in the key areas of competition, environment and energy policy, but more widely, too;

(3)   balancing the traditional supply-side orientation of energy policy with more explicit attention to energy efficiency;

(4)   greater policy attention to trends in energy demand, especially for transport, over the next two decades;

(5)   a comprehensive and regularly up-dated energy resource assessment for the UK; and, finally,

(6)   mechanisms to reconcile narrow, private corporate interests and wider national interests in specific strategic areas such as the large power generation fuel market.

REFERENCES

1.   White Paper on *Fuel Policy*, Ministry of Fuel and Power, HMSO, London, 1967, Cmnd 3438.

2.   *Energy Policy – A Consultative Paper*, (The Green Paper), Department of Energy, HMSO, London, 1978, Cmnd 7101.

3.   Where the RPI is the Retail Price Index, X measures internal operational efficiency gains, and Y is a measure of input fuel costs which may be passed through in full or in part.

4.   *This Common Inheritance – Britain's Environmental Strategy*, Department of the Environment, HMSO, London, 1990, Cm 1200, para. 1.6.

5.   *The Development of The Oil and Gas Resources of the United Kingdom*, Department of Energy, HMSO, London, (annual).

5 The Financial Condition of Energy Industries

I Canadian Oil and Gas Industries

William Gobert

Editorial note: Mr Gobert presented a statistical analysis, illustrated by the following figures.

Figure 1   Well Completions by Category

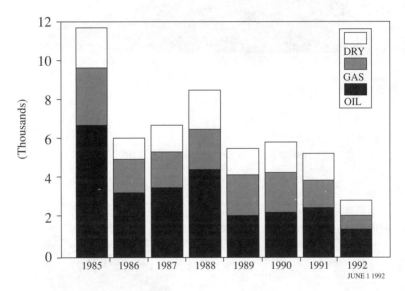

Source: Daily Oil Bulletin

Figure 2   US Oil Production (mmb/d)

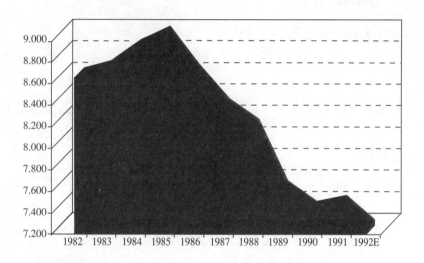

Figure 3   US Oil imports (Million B/D)

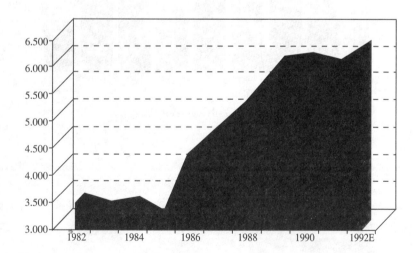

Figure 4   Operated Well Completions, Canada, 1985

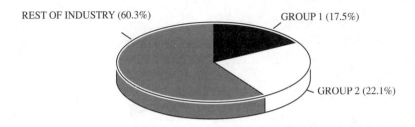

GROUP I: IMPERIAL, TEXACO, AMOCO, DOME,
MOBIL, CANADIAN SUPERIOR, HUSKY, CANTERRA
GROUP II: GULF, PETRO-CANADA, PANCANADIAN, ALBERTA ENERGY,
BP CANADA, HOME, CHEVRON, NORCEN, SHELL, CANADIAN HUNTER

Figure 5   Operated Well Completions, Canada, 1991

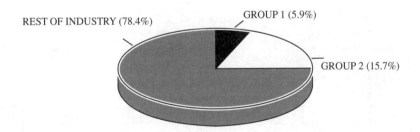

GROUP I: IMPERIAL, TEXACO, AMOCO, DOME,
MOBIL, CANADIAN SUPERIOR, HUSKY, CANTERRA
GROUP II: GULF, PETRO-CANADA, PANCANADIAN, ALBERTA ENERGY,
BP CANADA, HOME, CHEVRON, NORCEN, SHELL, CANADIAN HUNTER

Figure 6   USA Gas Supply (Trillion Cubic Feet)

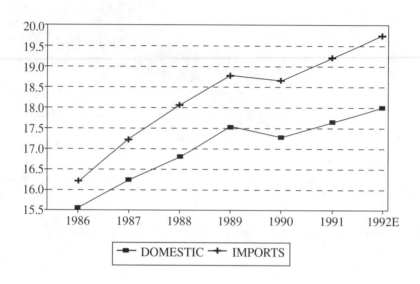

Figure 7   US Oil and Gas Energy Consumption
(per unit GNP – US$1982)

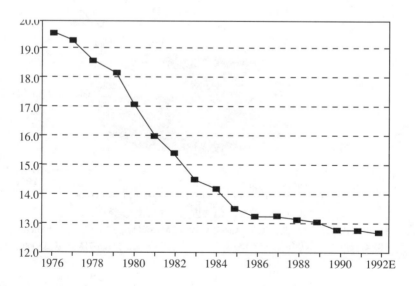

Figure 8 Proved Gas Reserves (Trillion Cubic Feet)

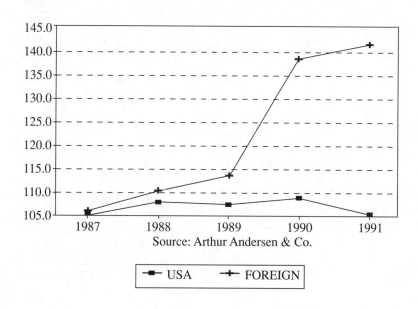

Source: Arthur Andersen & Co.

Figure 9 Oil and Gas Revenues ($US billions)

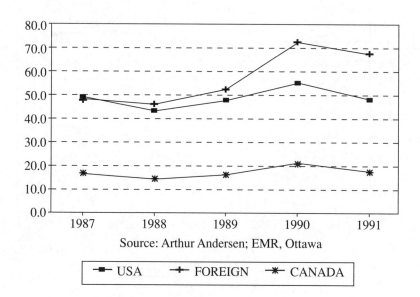

Source: Arthur Andersen; EMR, Ottawa

Figure 10   Oil and Gas Profits ($US billions)

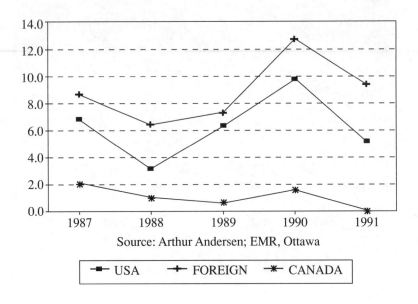

Source: Arthur Andersen; EMR, Ottawa

Figure 11   Gas Production (Trillion Cubic Feet)

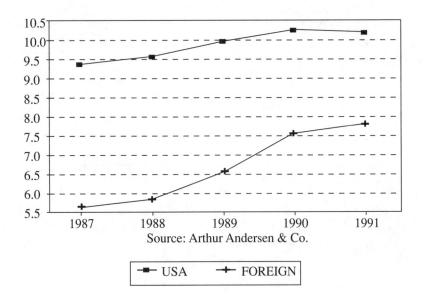

Source: Arthur Andersen & Co.

Figure 12 E&D Capital Expenditures (Billion Dollars)

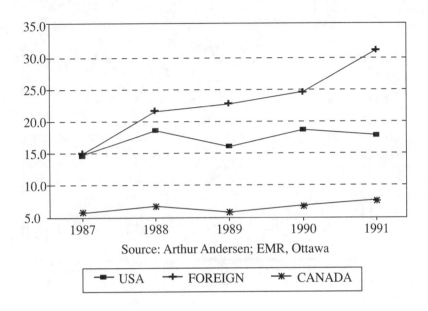

Source: Arthur Andersen; EMR, Ottawa

Figure 13 Proved Oil Reserves (Billion barrels)

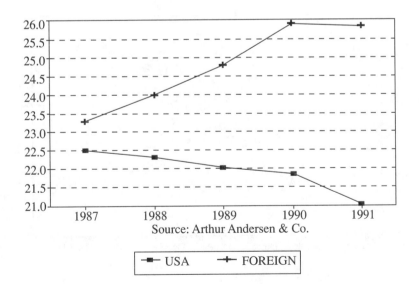

Source: Arthur Andersen & Co.

Facing the Energy Challenge

Figure 14   Nymex WTI Crude Oil (First Forward Month)

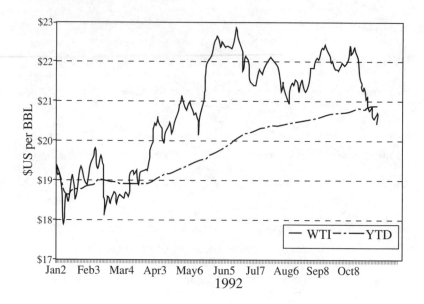

Figure 15   Canadian-US Exchange Rate (Monthly Average – US$)

FIGURE 16   NYMEX WTI CRUDE OIL
(Monthly average, US$/Barrel)

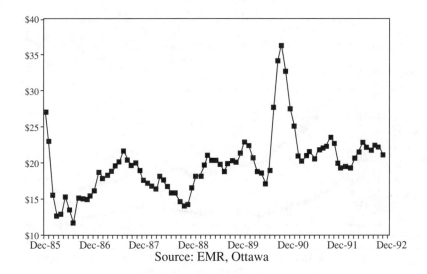

Source: EMR, Ottawa

Figure 17   Average Market Price (AMP) (Cdn$ per MMBTU)

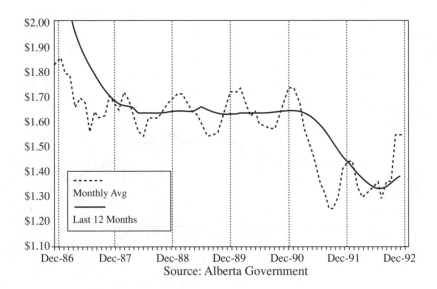

Source: Alberta Government

Facing the Energy Challenge

Figure 18   Canadian Gas Exports (Average Border Price)

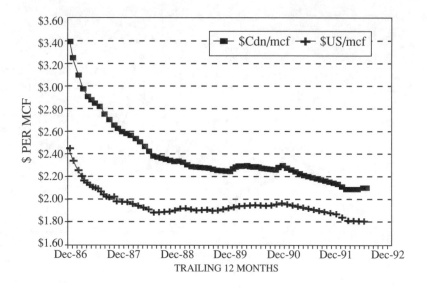

Figure 19   US Spot Wellhead (US$/Mcf)

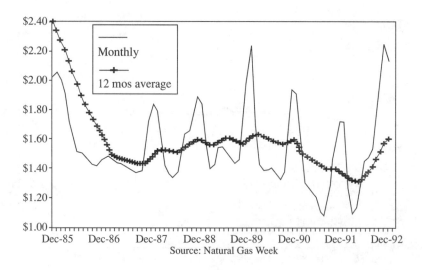

Figure 20 Gas Export Volumes (Last 12 Months – Bcf)

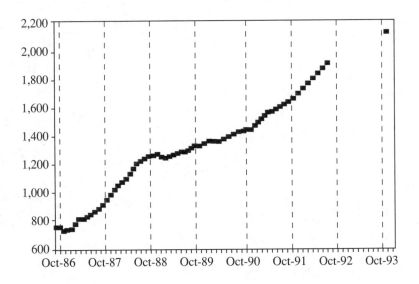

Figure 21 Canadian Gas Exports (Annual Revenue)

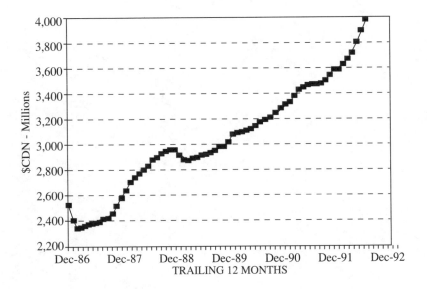

5 The Financial Condition of Energy Industries

II Global Conditions and Structural Problems

Christopher Cragg

It is hardly news that the world's energy industries are suffering from the global recession. The evidence is widely available. The oil majors, for example, have been undergoing extensive restructuring for three years now, marching back to the core business of finding, refining and selling oil and gas. The estimated job losses in the US oil sector alone is 50,000 in 1992. In the UK, BP has slimmed down substantially over the past few years. Somewhat erroneously this process has been seen as the consequence of the chairmanship of Bob Horton, yet it has continued under David Simons. BP may be a special case with a gearing ratio of over 80%, which makes the cut in its investment levels essential. As a result its planned spending in 1993–94 will be only $5 billion, or 37% less than in 1991.

Shell, probably the oil multinational with the best corporate public relations, has been in the middle of a major management shake-out, only they do not talk about it. Shell has now gone beyond the original 15% cut in jobs, decided in mid-1991. Capital expenditure in the first half of 1992 was 17% below that in 1991. Shell too is trimming its expenditure. Its net income in 1991 was 34% down on the 1990 result.

Chevron fared even worse, with a 40% drop in the same period. In mid-1992, only one US independent exploration and production company ranked above the lowest Standard and Poors category of BBB. Of course, it is not all bad news, Exxon bucked the trend to increase its 1991 earnings by 12% above the 1990 level. Nonetheless the direction has been clear for some time. The Seven Sisters are not what and who they were and the independent sector is no better and is probably worse.

Yet the multinationals are not the only one to be worried about cash-flow. If you define the average price of a barrel of oil at $33.7 in 1980 and then adjust that figure in 1980 dollars to the oil price in August this year, then the figure comes out at $14.8 per barrel in 1980 dollars and rather less for the Opec crudes. In effect, if you define the price of a barrel of oil in 1980 at 100, it is now at about 40 (see table, pp.114–5).

Of course the real damage on the oil front was done in 1985, when everybody had been riding high at an indexed figure of 154 for Opec crudes and only marginally less than 100 for many others. It was the events of 1986 that really hit the oil producers and in indexed terms, the Gulf war only returned matters to just over $21 a barrel in 1980 money.

Table   OPEC: Real prices and 'purchasing power' of crude oil

Year	Average price	Real price[1]	Real Purchasing power of a barrel		
			OPEC	M.-E.	Africa
I – In S/b. base 1980					
1978	14.6	18.5	20.3	19.6	20.2
1979	20.0	22.2	22.9	22.5	22.7
1980	33.7	33.7	33.7	33.7	33.7
1981	34.0	35.1	41.6	40.6	42.5
1982	31.5	33.5	45.3	44.1	46.3
1983	28.2	31.0	46.0	44.4	47.0
1984	27.6	31.4	52.0	49.0	53.4
1985	27.4	31.8	46.5	51.6	56.1
1986	13.2	13.5	18.3	17.2	18.7
1987	16.8	16.2	19.0	17.9	19.3
1988	14.0	12.8	13.6	13.2	13.8
1989	17.0	15.6	17.4	17.5	18.7
1990	21.3	18.3	17.4	17.8	18.7
1991	17.8	14.6	15.0	15.2	16.2
90/4	29.3	22.7	21.3	21.7	22.9
91/1	18.4	14.4	13.8	13.9	14.7
91/2	16.5	14.0	15.0	15.1	16.1
91/3	17.7	15.0	16.1	16.3	17.4
91/4	18.6	15.1	15.2	15.4	16.4
92/1	16.3	13.2	13.3	13.4	14.3
92/2	18.3	14.7	14.7	14.8	15.8
July 92	19.1	15.4	14.3	14.5	15.4
Aug 92	18.5	14.8	13.6	13.8	14.5

[1] Price in US dollars of a typical barrel of OPEC crude divided by the price of manufactured goods exported by the OECD to OPEC.

Given all the fuss at the time, this comes as a slight surprise. In fact the real lesson of the Gulf war was not in crude prices but in product prices. The crude price was controlled by the crude stockpile. The product price was controlled by the lack of refining capacity and the sheer volume of jet kerosene that the US Air Force was burning up over Kuwait. This did not last and indeed its net effect was to leave around 3 million barrels a day overhanging the crude market, since Iraq was no longer allowed its quota within Opec.

Table   OPEC: Real prices and 'purchasing power' of crude oil

Year	Average price	Real price[1]	Real Purchasing power of a barrel		
			OPEC	M.-E.	Africa
II – In indeces: base 1980=100					
1978	43.3	54.9	60.2	58.2	59.9
1979	59.3	65.9	68.0	66.8	67.4
1980	100.0	100.0	100.0	100.0	100.0
1981	100.9	104.2	123.4	120.5	126.1
1982	93.5	99.4	134.4	130.9	137.4
1983	83.7	92.0	136.5	131.8	139.5
1984	81.9	93.2	154.3	145.4	158.5
1985	81.3	94.4	138.0	153.1	166.5
1986	39.2	40.1	54.3	51.0	55.5
1987	49.9	48.1	56.4	53.1	57.3
1988	41.5	38.0	40.4	39.2	40.9
1989	50.4	46.2	51.6	52.1	55.6
1990	63.2	54.3	51.8	52.8	55.4
1991	52.8	43.4	44.6	45.0	48.0
90/4	86.8	67.5	63.2	64.5	67.9
91/1	54.5	42.8	40.9	41.3	43.7
91/2	49.1	41.6	44.4	44.9	47.9
91/3	52.6	44.6	47.8	48.3	51.7
91/4	55.1	44.7	45.2	45.7	48.7
92/1	48.5	39.2	39.4	39.8	42.5
92/2	54.4	43.6	43.6	44.0	46.9
July 92	56.8	45.6	42.6	43.1	45.7
Aug 92	54.9	44.0	40.3	40.8	43.1

[1] Price in US dollars of a typical barrel of OPEC crude divided by the price of manufactured goods exported by the OECD to OPEC.

Such indexed figures do indeed put the current oil market in perspective. The last time I was in Calgary, the effects of the events of 1986 were all too apparent. The crisis over Dome Petroleum was on and I remember the first man I met in Canada was a Sikh taxi driver who told me he was a redundant oil reservoir engineer.

Since then, of course, the situation has stabilised at around 43 as an indexed figure compared with 100 in 1980. In effect, the price of oil in real terms is rather less than half of what it was at the beginning of the last decade and we are, we hope, at the bottom of the cycle. Nonetheless, if the crash of 1986 was the beginning of this downward spiral, it did at least produce an annual increase in OECD GDP. Unhappily, we now have the worst of both worlds in that the post 1986 boom has blown itself out and we are in a serious recession. If there is anything to be learnt here, it is that any economic recovery worldwide cannot be fuelled by crude prices falling further.

Using the International Energy Agency's figures, we have indeed had an increase of demand for crude since 1988, when it was 64.9 million barrels a day (mbd). The IEA put average global demand at 67 mbd for 1992, giving an annual increase of only 3.2% in demand, over four years. With Opec improving its input from 21.7 mbd to around 26 mbd (including NGLs) in this time frame, there has been a squeeze on western multinationals, since Opec has provided for considerably more than the growth in the market. Yet as noted, shifts in currency markets have not brought Opec any real reward for this increase. Both sides of the old divide have suffered.

It is a matter of some dispute how far crude prices work their way into the prices of other energy sources. In Western Europe, natural gas prices tend to be indexed against petroleum products and occasionally coal and other pricing indexes. In the US, as Canada knows to its cost, the combination of a regulatory framework of enormous complexity, with an historical excess of gas – the gas bubble – has kept spot gas prices at historically low levels, while simultaneously, apparently, failing to get it into the marketplace. Here the rival fuel is undoubtedly heating oil, so the declining real cost of crude has also had an effect. The US situation has been much discussed, not least because 1992 average natural gas spot prices have been much too low to tempt many to drill in the lower 48 states.

What is less understood is that European border prices on long-term contracts have been sliding too. In April 1990, the Dutch were getting $2.69 per MMbtu; by September 1992, this was $2.54 per MMBtu. The only appreciable gainer in this period in Europe was the CIS exporter which shunted up the prices from the laughably low $1.77 per MMbtu to $2.42 – a matter of considerable significance for the future. Elsewhere there has been a slow downward drift.

Matters are not much better in the coal marketplace. Most energy economists would agree that the really dominant force in coal prices is the availability of US export coal as a swing producer in the marketplace. Equally however, it does suffer from the same oil impact in power generation where heavy fuel oil competes for market share. The news here has not been very happy over the past two years. An indexed average price, used by McCloskey Coal Information Services, for 1% sulphur, CIF Western Europe puts the decline at roughly $6 per tonne since January 1991, to roughly $35.50 per tonne, now.

This has not produced an easy time for mining profits, indeed Alberta recently changed its royalty system to take account of the new realities. In places like New South Wales, Australia, it has been seriously questionable whether anyone in coal mining is really making money. Westmoreland, one of the US coal companies, recorded a loss in 1991 for the first time since 1987 and is now being restructured. Part of the problem here has been the speed and high volumes suddenly produced on the market by new entrants like Colombia, Venezuela and Indonesia.

One cloud on this horizon is that CIF prices for coal are going to have to rise over the next five years. Current freight rates at around $9 a tonne for a Capesize vessel from Richard's Bay in South Africa to Japan are simply inadequate to amortize a new vessel. The Capesize bulk fleet is getting very elderly and a new vessel needs a rate of around $20 a tonne to make any sense at all. Similar problems are looming in the crude tanker market. Tanker rates in the first half of 1992 were half of what they were in the first half of 1992. It is the usual problem. Owners cannot afford to buy new ships at current freight rates, while scrap prices are low. To remain in business the owners are keeping their elderly ships afloat and in the market. We are clearly moving into the usual boom and bust cycle here.

It is worth noting that the state of the bulk shipping and tanker markets for these are just the extreme examples of the investment cycle in energy. This investment cycle does not necessarily follow pricing patterns of the oil market with any precision. For example, the tanker market's current problem is associated with the original boom in ordering prior to the 1973 oil price hike. The VLCCs and ULCCs that currently keep rates uneconomic were expensive because they were bought when yards were full. Ironically, post-1973 and the collapse of oil consumption, the market was full of new vessels that had arrived in 1975. Now, 16 years on, these are preventing the building of new vessels, except where environmental legislation demands it. Consequently, we are likely to see a higher increase in new building costs when the vessels are finally scrapped, than is really necessary.

The shipping market has a particularly lunatic swing, but what is true for ships is only slightly less true for drilling rigs and to a lesser extent for offshore oil capacity. The North Sea is currently coming to the end of a boom period of investment that was really predicated on prices prior to the 1986 collapse (and on tax changes even earlier). Take Shell's Eider Field. This is a small North Sea development to produce 45,000 barrels a day, in 500 ft of water and 119 miles from Shetland. The actual oil bearing rock formation was found in 1976. Appraised in 1978 and again in 1983, conceptual design started in 1984 and the scheme got government approval in 1985. The first oil started to flow in 1989. Shell was not slow in using design to lower costs and Eider used satellite platform design. As the company proudly pointed out, the design meant that 'production is now viable from a deep water field which would previously have been regarded as marginal.'

Yet the odd thing is that Eider's 45,000 barrels a day would have earnt $1.3 million a day in 1983 at the design stage and only $765,000 a day in 1989 when the oil started to flow. And since this is in money of the day terms, the real return per day from Eider was in practice around 50% of the expected cashflow when it was designed.

Eider is not particularly special, but it does reveal the spectacular difference between the expectation and the reality of reward in real terms, that has been the lot of oil companies in the past decade. This, one could say is just part of the risk-bearing that has to be taken. If construction takes a long time, the world does not sit still and wait to give you the rate of return you expected. Yet these projects are getting ever more capital intensive and taking longer to put together.

Take the Troll/Sleipner field complex, in the Norwegian sector. This is the development on which the supply of gas to western Europe is predicated, with deliveries starting in 1996 and most of the options taken up. Troll was discovered in 1979 and will actually reach peak production in 2002. The complex networks of pipelines, plus the field platforms, are going to cost Nkr 60 billion, or roughly $10 billion, or at least they were until Statoil managed to drop the 110 metre concrete Sleipner A base onto the floor of Stavanger fiord, causing a bang that registered 2.9 on the Richter scale.

This is no mean amount of capital investment, but it has to be put in the context of a total Norwegian offshore investment to maintain current oil output as well as to address Europe's gas shortages at $35 billion between 1991 and 1996. Yet one of the little known aspects of Norwegian policy is that it is the State's Direct Financial Participation (SDFP) that is really investing a large proportion of this money in return for production sharing rights. In practice, a very large amount of the downside risk is now born by the Norwegian state. There may well be nothing wrong with this, but it has to be said that without this financial input, it is extremely unlikely that either the banks or the oil companies would pick up this risk in the current atmosphere. And yet if they did not, then it is highly likely that the pattern of Norway's investment, so necessary to OECD oil output and Europe's gas supply, would not go ahead at the planned speed because of a shortage of capital.

On the UK side of the North Sea median line, we are now beginning to see the recessionary part of the cycle develop. The post-1986 reality of falling real oil prices is making itself felt in new platform orders and the rig rates are falling. Keeping up momentum has been greatly facilitated by the switch to gas in the UK electricity sector. Indeed, so far, the role of the oil companies in the shut-down of the UK coal industry has yet to be really told. It is, however a substitution policy, rather than a consequence of increased demand or of rising prices. Indeed, if the process of switching to gas for generation is stopped, there will be problems in the UK North Sea.

There are however two other major factors at work in the economics of energy at present that are increasingly important. Prior to the recent recession, the late 1980s brought two new ideological obsessions into the general marketplace. The first was the environmental movement; the second was the drive to make energy prices more responsive to market forces, even in energy systems like gas and electricity supply that had formerly acted as quasi monopolies. Oddly these two themes had a considerable element of contradiction in them. Obviously, the market mechanism for improving pollution was to make energy supply more expensive. However, price transparency and competitive forces, predicated on the market forces approach, was aimed at bringing them down. This contradiction was not, perhaps, sufficiently noted at the time. On the one side, those in favour of market forces pointed to the economic growth benefits of reducing prices through competition. Those in favour of an improved environment pointed to carbon taxes to bring them down.

During that affluent period, there did indeed seem a considerable need to clean up energy supplies, a process that culminated in the Rio conference and the obsession with global warming and cutting carbon emissions. Yet if carbon taxes are still in the background as a threat to energy costs, the environmental movement has substantially increased energy industry costs already. The chief targets here have been sulphur and nitrous oxides, or SO_x and NO_x. The problem affects virtually all energy sectors. Coal burning for power production is increasingly possible only with flue-gas desulphurization. At its current stage of technology, this is not only expensive, up to a third of the cost of the plant in terms of retrofitting, but de-rates a 1000 MW plant by up to 70 MW.

The reformulation of gasoline and diesel, to reduce not only sulphur and nitrogen product, but particulate and cancer-causing benzenes, is extremely expensive in terms of refinery upgrading. One IEA survey put the cost of reducing diesel sulphur to 0.05% at $1.2 billion per annum (running costs) and $3.3 billion in capital expenditure within its area. The same survey, put total oil company emission standard controls at $25–$29 billion annually in running expenditure and around $40 billion in new capital investment. Yet there were many blanks on the costings for matters concerning benzene emissions, volatilities, tank and pipe emissions, offshore effluent controls and new safe injection rules etc which are already at legislation stage in California. These are assumed to be coming to Western Europe and other places soon. To quote the chairman of Mobil, not so long ago: 'We are not leaving the US, we are being thrown out.'

Things might be easier if there were uniform agreement about the value, or at least the chemistry of reformulated gasoline, but the central point is the same for flue gas desulphurization as it is for barbecue controls in California: There is rarely an additional return on capital from new environmental regulation. On the contrary, per thermal unit bought, the costs are higher and the amount of crude or coal used to produce it is likely to be greater.

Of course, the energy producers and suppliers do not hesitate to exaggerate the threat of environmental regulation, a process known in some quarters as 'greenplating'. Yet it is there none the less. And it is equally the case that traditional energy suppliers like oil companies are now under threat – in relation to the environment – from other types of supply that may well have hidden subsidies. In Europe, for example, the diesel market is being marginally nibbled away by rapeseed oil, while ethanol is being actively considered. In California, we have the zero emission – i.e. electric – vehicle. One unpleasant fact here is that refined oil products are not endlessly interchangeable. If the Scandinavians insist on diesel specifications that mean a high use of jet kerosene, then the aviation fuel business has to use less environmentally sound material. If western users insist on straight run, low sulphur heavy fuel oil then somebody else gets left with the rerun crud from the bottom of the barrel.

All this might not matter if the price of the raw material was guaranteeing greater profitability, but as we have seen, the rate of return on oil production has fallen rapidly over the years. There is decreasing fat to be used on upgrading refineries if margins are extremely tight. Governments however still have a mental image of the oil industry as a tax cow, even when it is obvious that their current profitability is sustained mostly by the disposal of assets and redundancies.

It is perhaps a misfortune that the business of environmental regulation should be in full upswing, when the energy business, particularly oil, is at the bottom of its capacity for new investment. Yet the second point about the late 1980s trend towards greater competition adds to the same effect. In Europe, the EC emphasis on deregulation, unbundling and competition policy is beginning to have a serious impact on long-term planning. So far, outside the UK, the trend has not caught on outside the Competition Directorate of the Commission and it is most unlikely that the governments of France, Italy and Germany will allow third party access to triumph, if it might affect great institutions like Electricité de France. Indeed, senior power and gas executives from continental Europe and indeed Ireland cannot point to the UK experience without a serious belly laugh.

None the less, EC competition law is being rapidly increased, case by case. Ruhrgas is in a 'bloody' battle – their word – with Wintershall over the future of the European gas market. Their top executives seem to spend more and more time in federal courts, when perhaps all eyes really ought to be turned on the state of the Russian supply system. There are genuine fears that Europe may be developing a regulated market like that provided by the FERC in the US. The constant intervention of the gas regulator in the UK has reduced British Gas to a shadow of its former arrogant self, by the simple expedient of setting an allowable rate of return through regulation. This is not exactly what Adam Smith had in mind by the free market.

Of course, it is no bad thing to control monopolies. Yet the systematic use of competition law to reduce the giants of the industry down to size does have an impact on questions of supply security for the longer term. This is a question that has not been discussed much in the 1980s. Indeed our general complacency on the issue has been fuelled by the very slide in real energy prices that has substantially reduced our 'war chest' of capital necessary to do anything about it, should there be another crisis.

We have been here before. Peter Odell, hardly a man who believed in the scarcity of oil, pointed out in 'The future of Oil' that the 1960s oil company view of low-priced oil was so unsustainable that it was ridiculous. This was then followed by a period when everybody said that oil was rapidly running out. In fact, the simple key was that reserves were a function of price as much as availability. Now, after six years of declining real prices, we are probably yet not quite at the bottom of the cycle, but the demands made on the companies from other regulatory issues like environmentalism will quicken it, probably reaching the level where a rapid increase in energy prices is needed in the late 1990s, for investment reasons.

It is true that the energy economy is much more diversified than it was in the 1970s, but the interrelationship between all energy prices can bring surprises. It is the length of the investment cycle that does this. Take, for example, England's last fossil fuel power station, prior to the new gas investment. The Isle of Grain was a 2000 MW oil-fired station. Its foundations were being laid just as the Egyptians went over the Suez Canal at the time – 1973 – of Yom Kippur. It was completed in 1976 and has remained hardly in use since then; a monument to mistaken assumptions of price forecasters. Yet it was used in a period of great national crisis. For a few crucial months of the 1984–5 UK Miners strike, it was on permanent base-load supply. In combination with other UK oil-fired capacity, it kept Mrs Thatcher in power. Yet it also increased the UK oil burn by 600,000 bd at maximum, reversed the European refining system and may partially have been responsible for a temporary increase in the value of the dollar and the 1986 oil price debacle. Yet had the planners adhered strictly to the concept of marginal costs, it would never have been built at all. Indeed, for much of its life, it has been a hopelessly wrongheaded investment.

The Troll field, the Isle of Grain power station and indeed any nuclear capacity at all, are all long-term investments and assume risk-taking over a time scale that probably exceeds the cycle of oil prices. Of course, one does not need to assume that oil history is entirely circular. Nonetheless, three final points should be made. The first is that energy crisis does not necessarily always happen in oil, nor relate to middle eastern wars. Any commotion in Russia could now do similar things to western Europe. If gas supply security ceased, this would in turn very rapidly impact on gasoil prices and thus onto gasoline and diesel markets worldwide.

Yet secondly, we may not have reached the bottom of the fall in real energy prices, even though oil company resources for investment are at an all time low in real terms. One pistol shot in Iraq could start the process of dumping a further 3 million barrels a day on an already glutted market, with catastrophic effects on revenues and thus on investment decisions for the late 1990s.

And finally, in the context of the energy industries on the stockmarkets of the world, it has to be said that share markets are not driven by falling real rates of return, but by competitive purchase prices and dividends. By and large the stockmarkets of the world have been demanding in dividends the seedcorn money that should, perhaps, provide the investment money of the future. The result is perhaps best shown by BP, which financed its last dividend level partly by borrowing, because it was scared that pension funds, with a time horizon of five minutes, would make it vulnerable to takeover if it did not keep fund managers happy. (One partial benefit of the fall in real oil prices has been the abrupt departure of the Boone Pickens and the greenmailers who so very nearly did for Phillips Petroleum, on the fatuous grounds that profits did not adequately reflect oil reserves in the ground at pre-1986 prices.)

As we move out of the hang-over of the late 1980s, it is worth recalling a recent speech in London by a senior Chase Manhattan banker. Asked to answer to the question: 'Why on earth would anybody buy a Coal Mine?', he had a neat reply. He stuck up a slide and said, 'you need to look at the alternatives'. On the slide was a list of such alternatives. They were all highly speculative, not to say implausible, investments. As we go into 1990s, we should prepare for the rebound in energy prices, because it will surely come. Under current circumstances we are dangerously low on the necessary capital to meet the challenge.

6 Strategies for the Future

I   Research and Development – Alberta

William J. Yurko

I have been asked to give you a few comments on strategies for the future. Before I do that, I would like to comment a little on some of the situations we find ourselves in, as that will set the basis for future direction.

Perhaps the dominant influences on Research and Development today are the dramatic changes which are taking place in the business community. While I speak mainly from knowledge of the oil and gas industry, I suspect these changes are more broadly based. The introduction of quality management concepts, and in particular the reorganization of major companies into business units with the imperative that each business unit must show a profit, has reduced the pools of funds that are available for research both within and outside the corporation. Each individual business unit must show a profit and as a result is only interested in funding short-term research efforts – in reality service work – rather than exploratory or development research. The second trend in the industry is a marked decrease in individual corporate interest in being competitive in technological innovation and ownership; instead competition is shifted to technology application and resource opportunities. This does not mean corporations are any less interested in new technology, but they are much more willing to see it developed collectively and are less concerned in maintaining a corporate proprietary interest.

These two trends have had a dramatic effect on research in the oil and gas industry. Firstly, there has been a major down-sizing of corporate laboratories and/or a conversion of their activities to service laboratories for other business units within the company. Secondly, there has been a major growth of interest in joint research consortia whose goals are in the strategic interest of the companies. Examples of this are the Oil and Gas Forums which have sprung up in Canada and the U.S.A. Here research proposals are put on the table by companies or public research organizations in a sort of buffet fashion, and companies group themselves to support them according to their interest. Another example is the large commitment to joint research programs such as the 4,000,000/year jointly-funded research program being conducted at the Alberta Research Council. To be successful such programs must focus on areas of strategic interest to a large number of companies and be involved in high-risk, innovative and exploratory research. I must confess, however, that I have some concern about this research trend, as too often joint research is run by joint committees. This often leads to agreement on the lowest common denominator which stifles the innovation that is so important to success.

One of the ways to encourage innovation and diversity of thought is to involve the academic community in the process. For a number of years, AOSTRA has operated a university research program which has successfully harnessed some of the tremendous resources available at universities and directed them towards the problem of oil sands recovery and processing. This program has seen a dramatic growth in work by university scientists and engineers across Canada into the real technological challenges the oil sands present rather than the more esoteric problems they are accustomed to. It has had the added benefit of training a lot of people for the industry; not only have hundreds of graduate students been trained and gone out into the industry, but an interested academia has fostered numerous undergraduate and graduate courses. An important feature of this program has been the close co-operation between government, industry and the academic community.

I am aware of an EEC (European Economic Community) study on factors affecting economic growth. The study looked at countries around the world and tried to identify common factors for growth. Two factors stood out: discipline and a practical knowledge of technology. Certainly in Germany and Japan these factors are very apparent. You only have to board a subway in Tokyo or see a Japanese engineer at work on the production floor to see both in action. For my part I have travelled extensively in the Soviet Union, when it still was the Soviet Union, and was impressed by the excellent science and academic technology that existed but at the same time depressed at the application of the technology. One of the major breakthroughs in bitumen recovery has been the application of steam-assisted Gravity Drainage from Underground Access – a technology which was pioneered in the Soviet Union but has not been widely used due to poor application. In Latin America while the numbers of good scientists and engineers is much smaller, the unwillingness to get actively involved with technology – to get your hands dirty – is even more apparent. Kalvin is quoted as saying 'if you can't measure something you don't understand it'. I think it is equally true that if you can't apply technology or work with it, you don't understand it.

AOSTRA, in addition to its University Research work, has sought in its training programs to give practical experience where possible. We have strongly supported University Co-op programs, given summer employment to students in field and laboratory settings and provided industrial post-doctoral fellowships to encourage our best to get out and obtain practical experience.

So successful has the co-op program been with the University of Waterloo in Ontario that Alberta is often jokingly referred to as having three major Universities – Alberta, Calgary and Waterloo – since so many of the latter's students obtain their practical, on-the-job training there.

I noted earlier the shift by industry to competition in the application of technology. In many ways AOSTRA has been ahead of this trend. The bulk of its funds have been spent on joint field projects with industry both at the test-pilot and demonstration stage. These joint projects have led directly to three commercial ventures and are demonstrating the commercial production of huge quantities of bitumen at costs as low as $7 Canadian/bbl. The AOSTRA approach is a highly effective model for Industry-Government co-operation. By working with industry in a cost-shared basis, and maintaining confidentiality and propriety interests where appropriate, the technology of bitumen extraction has been advanced dramatically. This mechanism has enabled industry to bring its best ideas forward, and to field-test and demonstrate these high-risk, high-potential prospects at an acceptable cost. Society will reap the rewards in an exploitable resource and in assured and lower-cost petroleum products.

Increasingly social issues require a knowledge of science and technology to be understood, and often also require technological solutions. In short, they require a technological culture. Can decisions really be made on issues such as the greenhouse effect or nuclear issues outside an understanding of the technology? In North America one of the disturbing trends is the move away from science and engineering and into the arts and humanities. Certainly, here in Alberta we have not done very well. A recent study conducted by the Alberta Chamber of Resources compared Alberta, Germany, Japan and Hungary. In all cases they found that Alberta delivered less mathematics and science to its students and in less depth at any given level than the other countries studied. Is it any surprise that fewer students go on to study science and engineering at university?

The lack of technological culture is evident at all levels from the extremely low expenditures in Canada on research and development to that section of society that looks at technology as the problem rather than the solution. Yet technology can be the solution. It is only necessary to drive by a modern refinery to know how far we have come in providing a clean environment while still meeting our energy needs. The application of clean coal technology through combined cycle power-generation facilities can nearly double our electrical power capacity for the same amount of CO_2 generated and remove SO_x and NO_x at the same time. The impact of that technology in a country like China would be enormous.

Public education on science and technology is imperative and it is for this reason that a number of Alberta agencies have banded together to get this message across. This group has taken media training, is working with the media on science specials, participating in science fairs, library programs and career shows as well as publishing promotional material.

I would now like to speak a little more directly of Alberta. The three major industrial sectors are agriculture, petroleum and forestry. In the petroleum sector we have relied for some time on the production of conventional oil but since 1973 this has been in decline. We have, however, an awesome reserve of bitumen locked in sand and carbonate deposits. Today we have the technology to produce vast amounts of that bitumen at costs as low as $7/bbl but the product produced is bitumen, not oil. The technology exists to convert that bitumen into oil but the costs, at $15 Canadian/bbl, are too high. One of our biggest research challenges today is to develop technology to get those costs down. If this is achieved, you will see rapid development of this resource with major plant construction, economic activity and employment.

In conclusion, I would like to say that Canada has huge resources. To date it has done very well by exploiting those resources. I believe future economic development and diversification will take place by building on that base through further processing of those resources. In Alberta we have awesome bitumen resources which must be partly processed before transportation to markets. Why not go all the way to transportation fuels? In most areas of the world the petrochemical industry is based on the refinery industry. Why not in Alberta?

We believe that despite the growth of alternate fuels and renewable resources, petroleum will form the backbone of the transportation fuel industry into the foreseeable future. Canada has vast quantities of natural gas and bitumen which taken together, and with the use of advanced technology, can provide environmentally acceptable transportation fuels well into the 21st century. Government must work with industry in the development and commercialization of the requisite technology.

6 *Strategies for the Future*

II Energy Efficiency Research and Development
in the United Kingdom

Gary J. K. Acres

INTRODUCTION

In my view there are at least four good reasons why the UK should invest
in energy efficiency R & D:

- economic;
- sustainable development;
- environmental;
- security of energy supply.

In the UK, we spend £50 billion each year on energy and we believe
that 20% of this consumption could be cost-effectively saved now. So the
scale of wastage, approximately £10 billion per annum, is very significant,
being equal to about 2% of our GDP. Secondly, partly to ensure that
scarce fossil fuel reserves are kept for future generations and as an
important step on the road to sustainable development, energy efficiency
has a very important role to play. Thirdly, getting more energy service
from each unit of energy will considerably reduce the environmental
damage which our current extraction and use of energy implies, in particular through the threat of global warming. Finally, more efficient use of
energy reduces dependence on imported fuel and recent events in the
Gulf have reminded us of the dangers of oil supplies and prices.

Past experience has shown that despite these benefits little progress is
made without government guidance, involvement and financial incentives, where appropriate. In my presentation I will highlight the approach
which the UK Government has taken over the past 14 years to energy
efficiency R & D and highlight a selection of the projects that form part
of the current programme.

Energy efficiency R, D and D was, until the recent reorganization of
government departments, the responsibility of the Department of Energy
and more specifically the Energy Efficiency Office (EEO) with the
support of a special unit, the Energy Technology Support Unit (ETSU).

From the beginning, particular emphasis was placed on exploiting
existing technology in applications featuring energy efficiency but including other benefits which would add to the overall returns of the investment.
The programme was known as the Energy Efficiency Demonstration
Scheme. As the title implies, the emphasis was on demonstrations in

127

practical situations of how energy could be used more effectively, quantifying these benefits as well as the financial returns as the basis for encouraging others to take up or replicate the technology. The Demonstration Programme also encouraged and supported R & D projects aimed at improving products, processes and materials. Reference to the slow rate of take up of energy efficient technology explains why this approach was taken.

The success of these schemes can be judged by the number of projects, the energy saved and the cost to government. For example, up to 1989 when the format of the schemes was changed, as I will explain later, 307 EEDS projects and 153 EER&D projects had been supported. Energy savings of 5 Mtce per annum worth £350M to UK Industry had been achieved. For each £1 invested by the UK Government £5 of energy savings had accrued.

Examples of projects will be illustrated ranging from brewing and whisky distilling through chemicals to pottery and the metals industry. Energy efficiency in buildings and houses is also included in the programme.

An important aspect of the success of these schemes was the adoption of a strategic approach. From an early stage, the importance of identifying energy usage by sector and opportunities for improving efficiency played a major part in selecting projects. When key projects were not forthcoming and considered necessary for the overall strategy they were actively promoted.

THE BEST PRACTICE PROGRAMME

In 1989 the programme was reviewed and the energy efficiency targets increased from 4.5 Mtce/year worth £350 million per annum to 9.0 Mtce/year worth over £700 million per annum. At the same time the programme was retitled The Best Practice Programme. This retained the main elements of the Demonstration Scheme but expanded its scope. The four main elements of the programme are:

Energy Consumption Guides

Energy Consumption Guides give data on the way in which energy is currently used in specific processes, operations, plant and building types. This information is gathered on an unattributable basis by asking a representative sample of organizations to provide energy data on the process, operation, plant or building by means of a simple questionnaire. The questionnaire returns are analysed and an Energy Consumption Guide prepared which provides organizations with sufficient information to compare their current usage with others in their sector or with others occupying similar building types.

Good Practice

Good Practice promotes examples of proven techniques which are already enabling the better energy users to be more energy efficient. Through its links with industrial and building professionals, the EEO disseminates impartial and authoritative information, either as guides or as case studies. To obtain the information needed to prepare the case studies and to assist in their promotion may require an additional effort on the part of the participating organization. In such cases, the EEO is prepared to consider making funds available – up to a maximum of £10,000 – to the organization to offset the costs of providing the information and facilitating/ co-operating in its dissemination.

The literature produced ranges from simple case studies to detailed guidance notes for the implementation of energy efficient methods and the installation of equipment. Independent consultants are employed to prepare case study material and to verify the energy savings by carrying out a short (typically two weeks' duration) technical audit of the practice.

New Practice

New Practice monitors first commercial applications of new energy efficient measures in order to obtain unbiased expert evaluations of those measures. The EEO recognises that to obtain information on new, unfamiliar energy saving measures is going to require considerable co-operation from the participating organization. The EEO is therefore prepared to consider making funds available – up to a maximum of £50,000 – to the organization to offset the costs of providing information to facilitate promotion of the measure if shown to be successful. Independent monitoring of the project is carried out by a monitoring contractor whose costs are paid by the EEO. The monitoring contractor prepares a report for publication. Projects may be promoted through a number of routes, including literature, site visits and seminars to accelerate the widespread acceptance of those measures and to promote their adoption as good practice. Projects considered for support are in the following main areas:

- novel technology;
- novel management techniques for encouraging
  improved energy efficiency;
- novel operation of plant;
- novel design techniques.

Future Practice: Research & Development

Future Practice supports joint ventures into new energy efficiency measures. Funding is available for basic R&D on new measures which could form the good practice of the future. Up to 49% of eligible costs could be available for organizations who enter into a joint project with the EEO. It is not intended that funding will be available for large single companies or organizations. Instead, projects should be of the multi-client type. Projects are envisaged in areas such as:

- technology;
- design;
- management methods;
- training.

BEST PRACTICE PROJECTS AND TRAINING

By way of examples of the Best Practice Programme I aim to give you an overview of the UK's current energy efficiency activities.

Furnace Technology

The Solstar computer-aided methoding and solidification simulation system for foundries has been the subject of Good Practice Case Studies in iron, steel and non-ferrous establishments. In April 1991, it earned its developers, Foseco Ltd, the Queen's Award for Technology and is now widely sold both in the UK and abroad.

The Pottery Industry

Staffordshire Tableware Ltd, winners of the 1990 National GEM Award, have replaced their two existing kilns with two open-flame, gas-fired tunnel kilns. A low thermal mass allows these kilns to be brought up to temperature in just one hour, resulting in primary energy savings of over 60% and a 7% increase in production. Additional cost savings derive from reductions in labour, maintenance and the use of refractory kiln furniture, and from quality improvements.

As well as a very successful event and site visit in February 1992, which promoted the technology to 140 pottery industry delegates, the technical and economic success of the project has been recognised by the presentation of a New Practice Certificate, the first of its kind, to the company's Managing Director.

Aerodynamic Trucks

Eye-catching, fuel-saving and cost-effective aerodynamic trucks have been the subject of two EEO-supported projects managed and extensively promoted by ETSU. As well as the distribution of over 7,000 publicity documents, the promotional campaigns have included twenty-one well attended regional evening workshops; three training courses, organised jointly with the Freight Transport Association; and a video entitled 'Box Clever', over 500 copies of which have been issued.

As a result of these activities, more than 300 aerodynamic trucks are already in service throughout the UK. Many of these are on trial in large fleets, offering the prospect of considerable future replication.

Aluminium Recycling

A novel aluminium recycling plant developed for J McIntyre (Aluminium) Ltd collected an impressive list of awards: the Queen's Award for Technological Achievement; the PA Golden Leaf Award for responsible environmental management; and a National GEM Award for new technology.

The plant can reprocess a wide range of scrap with a greatly improved yield and an energy consumption 65% less than most conventional furnaces. Emissions are removed by a sophisticated fume treatment system. Independent monitoring showed annual savings exceeding £1M with a payback of just 14 months.

Integrated CHP/Incinerator Unit

An integrated CHP unit and waste incinerator were installed at Queen Elizabeth Medical Centre in Birmingham at a cost of £2.35M, part-funded by the EEO and managed by ETSU.

Exhaust gases from the 3.6 MW dual-fuel gas turbine based unit (which can operate either in parallel with the grid or in 'island' mode) and the 750 kg/hour incinerator can be directed to a common waste heat boiler.

The integrated scheme has performed well, achieving cost savings of about £700,000/year with a payback of 3.4 years.

Best Practice Seminar

A well trained workforce is one of the keys to industrial energy efficiency, and Best Practice programme material produced by ETSU is now finding its way into training applications. During 1991/92, teaching material based on Best Practice CHP literature and produced for ETSU by Manchester Polytechnic has been on trial at about 30 higher education establishments. Its enthusiastic reception by lecturers and students alike is encouraging ETSU to make the material more widely available in 1992/93.

In another example, the Institute of British Foundrymen (IBF) has adopted Good Practice Guide 17 as part of the industry's professional training requirements: in addition, the IBF has asked ETSU to assist in shaping its training programme in 1992/93.

These are examples illustrating the application of technology to energy efficiency.

NEW PRACTICE R&D PROGRAMMES

Finally a brief outline of the current approach to determining the UK R&D programme on energy efficiency, a summary of subjects of current interest and examples of ongoing projects.

Selection and prioritization of R&D projects is always a challenge for both industry and government and energy efficiency is no exception in our experience. In the UK energy efficiency programme, a three step approach has been developed to progress ideas through a selection process to active support.

Topics for study are taken from many sources, usually the technical press or personal contact. These topic areas are then investigated to assess their energy efficiency potential. The depth of the assessment increases in three stages and, at each stage, the merits of the subject are compared with others. This ensures that the most promising areas are advanced, taking into account specific needs and developments at the time. This introduces considerable flexibility into the programme. Some subject areas may move quickly from the initial idea to active support of R&D. Others may be researched, but not progressed until later.

Areas of interest for current and future consideration include:

Ongoing Topics: Furnaces, Advances in Computing, Compact Heat Exchangers, Fuel cells for CHP, Instrumentation & Sensors and Process Intensification

Strategies: Ultrasound, Crushing, Membranes, Materials Selection Design & Forming

Strategic Briefings: Ceramic Heat Exchangers, Novel Low Temperature Heat Recovery Techniques and Energy Storage.

The following descriptions of ongoing projects illustrate the wide range of energy efficiency R&D projects in the UK.

Improved Recuperation in Furnaces and Kilns

Compact recuperative combustion systems are well established for high temperature processes (>1100°C). However, significant quantities of lower temperature waste heat could also be saved if similar technology was available to utilize this heat.

In this project a high performance recuperative system for processes in the 700–1100°C range is being developed. The work builds on the technology of current metallic recuperative burners which are well proven.

The system will be available as both a self-recuperative burner and as a separate recuperator. The system, with appropriate controls, is expected to achieve up to 30% energy savings.

Novel Heat Exchanger Surfaces

Compact heat exchangers offer high heat transfer surface areas within a small volume. However, the two main types (plate fin exchangers and printed circuit heat exchangers) both have limitations.

In this project an alternative type of enhanced surface for flat plate exchangers is being investigated, which offers benefits over the existing types. Basically, it is formed by layering flattened expanded metal sheets between the flat plates, thus giving a multitude of flow channels.

The project will investigate the thermal performance, pressure drop characteristics and ease of construction of the compact heat exchanger.

Heat Flux Probe in a Baking Oven

Due to the difficulties of accurate temperature measurement within ovens, bakers tend to experiment with oven settings until they find a point at which the product is acceptable. This means that the oven is probably not operating at optimum efficiency.

In this project a new heat flux probe, capable of giving a signal in proportion to the heat transferred to the product, will be installed on the three ovens ranging from pilot scale to full commercial size. The oven will be modelled so that optimum baking conditions can be predicted.

A better understanding of the measurement and control of oven working conditions should increase fuel efficiency by encouraging better energy efficient oven design and retrofit control systems for improved efficiency on existing ovens.

Expert Systems for Refrigeration System Selections and Diagnosis

While it is unusual for refrigeration equipment to fail completely, such plant becomes less efficient with time. As a result, electrical consumption steadily increases as staff tend to concentrate on more 'visible' problems.

This project aims to develop a quick and easy-to-use aid for engineering staff that will request information about the plant operation and give the user advice as to how to improve the plant performance. It will also be able to advise on the design of new refrigeration plant. Expert system technology will be used to allow this knowledge to be widely available on standard desktop computers.

Although the initial research will focus on the brewing industry, expert systems will be developed for wider applications in other business.

Fuel Cells for CHP

Fuel cells operated for CHP should give high fuel efficiencies with a high electricity/heat output. The possibilities for this aspect of fuel cells is being examined in relation to other initiatives.

OTHER NATIONAL ACTIVITIES

Within the UK there are several other initiatives which support R&D relevant to the activities of the Best Practice programme, although none is directly targeted towards developments in energy efficiency. The programmes of the Department of Trade and Industry (DTI) and the Science and Engineering Research Council (SERC) both encompass a number of project areas with a direct impact on energy efficiency. The DTI and SERC operate the LINK programme, which also involves energy efficiency-related co-ordinated projects.

The Department of Trade and Industry

Of particular interest to EEO activities is the activity of the Manufacturing Technology Division of DTI, described more fully in the Appendix. A number of active project areas in this Division complement the activities of the EEO, particularly in subjects such as compact heat exchangers and process intensification. There is a growth in the latter field that is also apparent within the SERC programme, which makes the strategy development role of ETSU particularly appropriate at this time.

The Science and Engineering Research Council

The SERC project portfolio includes programmes relevant to energy efficiency and provides the UK science base for more applied projects. Increased liaison between project managers within all these programmes is evident and encouraging. Examples of the types of projects which typify such SERC activities are also listed in the Appendix, and were taken from two important initiatives, Interfaces and Catalysis; and Separation Processes.

APPENDIX: DETAILS OF OTHER UK R&D INITIATIVES

The Department of Trade and Industry

The Manufacturing Technology Division of DTI has a number of sections, dealing with advanced manufacturing technology, materials, standards, metrology and engineering technology. Within the Engineering Technology Branch, MT3, there are seven sub-groups, one of which encompasses processing engineering. Process Engineering has a remit which includes several activities complementary to those of the EEO R&D programme.

The DTI strategy in this area includes the promotion of technologies for process efficiency, including process integration, process intensification, and high technology process equipment. Currently concentration is on process intensification and compact equipment, and in this activity close links have already been established with ETSU. Other strategic activities cover modelling and simulation, computational fluid dynamics, (where technology transfer is rated highly), and membranes.

Typical of the projects supported by DTI within MT3 is the £1.5 million contract recently placed with the Energy Environment Centre at NEL. The aim of the project is to develop a mathematical model for energy systems which can be used to optimize energy efficiency and environmental performance for real industrial processes. The model will be available in the form of a computer program, ACES, (Analysis of Clean Energy Systems). The five year project will cover the development of models for combustion and heat exchanger fouling, which will be incorporated in a process integration program capable of optimizing energy and environmental efficiency.

Details of SERC/LINK Activities Active During the Last Year

SERC Interfaces and Catalysis Initiative

Within the SERC Interfaces and Catalysis Initiative, described in the last Review of Non-EEO R&D Programmes, a number of new projects have been initiated under the collaborative LINK programme. Because of the recent growth in interest in catalytic combustion and related technologies in the context of energy efficiency, these projects are listed below.

- Oxide anodes for methane activation processes in ceramic electro-chemical reactors.
- Zeolite materials for novel cracking catalysts and for organic synthesis.
- Control of exhaust emissions from gasoline engines using novel non-precious metal/metal oxide catalysts.
- Selective production of oxygenated chemicals.
- Diesel emission control.
- Catalytic combustion.
- Modelling combustion non-adiabatic conditions in a catalytic monolith reactor for a gas turbine.

SERC Separation Processes Programme

A second area of SERC activity with a direct relevance to some aspects of the EEO Energy R&D programme is the separation processes initiative. This has been operating for a number of years, and has recently encompassed work on a number of 'enhanced' unit operations which could give energy and/or intensification benefits. To date the majority of projects have been supported outside the LINK programme, although industrial involvement is evident in some areas.

The topics covered are:

- – Membranes.
- – Liquid-Liquid Extraction.
- – Selective Adsorption.
- – Highly Selective Separations.
- – Centrifugal/Magnetic/Ultrasonic Fields.
- – Distillation.

7 *Postscript*

Michael Clark

It was an honour, and a great pleasure to take part in the Canada-UK Colloquium. The topic this year was 'Energy', and those of us who had the opportunity to attend and participate appreciated the presentations and the exchange of views that the format made possible.

It soon became clear that collectively participants had a broad knowledge of energy extending beyond local or national territories. Thus the Canadians were able to describe not only their own energy opportunities and challenges, but also those of North America as a whole. Similarly the British put the changing UK energy scene within the context of the European Community. In this way the colloquium was able to cover two of the world's three major trading blocks.

By the very nature of a residential colloquium relevant conversations took place outside the conference room. While walking, eating and relaxing, the participants exchanged experiences, information and – most interestingly of all – facts of political, parliamentary, constitutional and historic interest about their respective country. I feel certain that must be a prime objective of any international or bi-lateral gathering.

If we reached conclusions at all they revolved around price and long-term availability of energy, and environmental considerations.

Natural gas is being used increasingly, over the next 25 years its use will double and prices probably increase steeply. In the short term however, gas is plentiful and cheap, as are most energy sources. There seems little likelihood of firm national energy policies in these circumstances. It was however pointed out that energy policy is largely determined at arm's length by national policies on housing, social welfare, national security, transport and the environment.

The environment featured prominently in all discussions. It was pointed out that most developed countries are becoming more diligent in the introduction of measures to protect the environment. Often these expensive measures made only marginal improvement within the country concerned. We concluded that as the environment was a global matter the problem should be tackled world-wide. For example millions of dollars spent reducing CO_2 by increasing the thermal efficiency of western power stations, could be far more effectively used helping China to improve effectiveness of her numerous coal-burning power stations which apparently have efficiencies below 20%.

The meeting concluded with the politicians being charged to 'do something'. In response the politicians present retorted that they could tax and legislate, inform and lead, but priorities must be determined by the electorate; through open debate and consensus.

Appendix

British and Canadian Delegations to the
Canada-UK Colloquium, Kananaskis, November 1992

CANADIAN PARTICIPANTS

Pierre R. Alvarez
Secretary to the Cabinet and Deputy Minister to the Executive Council, Government of the Northwest Territories, previously Deputy Minister, Energy Mines and Resources

Gerry Angevine
President of the Canadian Energy Research Institute

Brian Davis
Manager, Public Affairs, Shell Canada

Peter Dobell
Secretary of the Institute for Research on Public Policy and Director of the Parliamentary Centre for Foreign Affairs and Foreign Trade

Wilfred A. Gobert
Principal and Director of Research for Peters & Co.

Ross Harvey, M.P.
New Democrat MP for Edmonton East, 1988– ; energy critic for the caucus

Daniel Phillip Hays
Senator 1984– , chair of Energy, Environment and Natural Resources Committee

Al Johnson, M.P.
MP for Calgary North 1988– ; chair of Standing Committee on Energy, Mines and Resources and the P.C. caucus committee on family issues

Roland Priddle
Chairman of the National Energy Board

John M. Reid, P.C.
President of the Canadian Nuclear Association since 1990. Representing Kenora Rainy River, 1965–1984, he also served as Minister responsible for Federal/Provincial Relations

Michael Ross Robertson
Senior Director, Environmental Health and Safety, Petro-Canada; previously Regional Director of the Canadian Wildlife Service in Western and Northern Canada

Mitchel P. Rothman
Chief Economist of Ontario Hydro, serving in the Economics & Forecasts Division of the Environment and Corporate Planning Branch

Glenn Wickerson
General Manager, Tax, for Amoco Canada Petroleum

Gil Winstanley
Director of International Energy Relations Division of Energy, Mines and Resources Canada; Canadian representative at the Governing Board of the International Energy Agency in Paris

William J. Yurko
Chairman and CEO of the Alberta Oil Sands Technology and Research Authority. As an Alberta MLA, 1967–1978, he served as Minister of Environment and Minister for Housing and Public Works. He was a Member of Parliament, 1979–1984

BRITISH PARTICIPANTS

Gary J.K. Acres
Director, Technology Planning, for the Johnson Matthey Research Centre

David Adams
Professor of American Studies at Keele University and Chair of the British Committee of the Canada-UK Colloquium

Kevin Barron
M.P. for Rother Valley, Yorkshire; former private secretary to Neil Kinnock and Labour spokesman for energy, 1989–92

Sir Nicholas Bayne KCMG
British High Commissioner to Canada, and formerly Deputy Under Secretary of State for Economic Affairs at the Foreign and Commonwealth Office

John Harvey Chesshire
Head of the energy program of the Science Policy Research Unit, University of Sussex

Michael Clark
M.P. for Rochford, Essex, since 1983 and chair of the all-Party Group for Energy Studies

Christopher T. Cragg
Editor of the *FT Energy Economist*, since 1983

Allan Hird
Executive Secretary of the Canada/U.K Colloquium

Anthony Joy
Consul General to British Columbia and Alberta since 1990. From 1976 to 1980, he was First Secretary (Energy) at the British Embassy, Washington D.C.

Roger Levett
CAG Consultants, formerly with Scottish Enterprise's Energy and Environmental Technologies Group

Karen Jane Sievewright
Materials Scientist with the Research and Technology Division of British Gas; currently on a year's secondment to TransCanada Pipelines

Mark Turner
Canada Desk Officer at the Foreign and Commonwealth Office

Malcolm Wesley
Executive Vice President, British Gas Holdings (Canada)

For a complete list of Ryburn and Keele University Press books in print, please write to Ryburn Distribution, Keele University, Staffordshire ST5 5BG, England